BILLY GRAHAM
Evangelistic Association
Always Good News.

W9-AWO-685

Dear Friend,

I am pleased to send you this copy of *Jesus + Nothing = Everything* by my nephew Tullian Tchividjian. Tullian is a pastor and author and frequently teaches at the Billy Graham Training Center at The Cove.

Are you trying to please God or men? In this book, Tullian shares that when we truly understand what Jesus did for us on the cross, we are freed from our failures and measuring ourselves by the opinions of others—so we can live boldly for Christ. *"'My grace is sufficient for you, for My strength is made perfect in weakness'"* (2 Corinthians 12:9, NKJV). I pray this book will point you to the One who loves you unconditionally: Jesus Christ.

For more than 60 years, the Billy Graham Evangelistic Association has worked to take the Good News of Jesus Christ throughout the world by every effective means available, and I'm excited about what God will do in the years ahead.

We would appreciate knowing how our ministry has touched your life. May God richly bless you.

Sincerely,

Franklin Graham
President

If you would like to know more about our ministry, please contact us:

IN THE U.S.:
Billy Graham Evangelistic Association
1 Billy Graham Parkway
Charlotte, NC 28201-0001
BillyGraham.org
info@bgea.org
Toll-free: 1-877-247-2426

IN CANADA:
Billy Graham Evangelistic
  Association of Canada
20 Hopewell Way NE
Calgary, AB T3J 5H5
BillyGraham.ca
Toll-free: 1-888-393-0003

JESUS

+

NOTHING

=

EVERYTHING

JESUS

+

NOTHING

=

EVERYTHING

TULLIAN TCHIVIDJIAN

This *Billy Graham Library Selection* special edition is published
with permission from Crossway Books.

::: **CROSSWAY**

WHEATON, ILLINOIS

Jesus + Nothing = Everything

©2011 by Tullian Tchividjian

Cover design: Dual Identity inc.

First printing 2011

Printed in the United States of America

Unless otherwise indicated, Scripture quotations are from the ESV® Bible (*The Holy Bible, English Standard Version*®), ©2001 by Crossway. Used by permission. All rights reserved.

Scripture quotations marked HCSB have been taken from *The Holman Christian Standard Bible*®. ©1999, 2000, 2002, 2003 by Holman Bible Publishers. Used by permission.

Scripture quotations marked MESSAGE are from *The Message*. ©by Eugene H. Peterson 1993, 1994, 1995, 1996, 2000, 2001, 2002. Used by permission of NavPress Publishing Group.

Scripture quotations marked NASB are from *The New American Standard Bible*®. ©The Lockman Foundation 1960, 1962, 1963, 1968, 1971, 1972, 1973, 1975, 1977, 1995. Used by permission.

Scripture quotations marked NCV are from *The Holy Bible, New Century Version*, ©1987, 1988, 1991 by Word Publishing, Dallas, Texas 75039. Used by permission.

Scripture references marked NIV are taken from The Holy Bible, New International Version®, NIV®. ©1973, 1978, 1984 by Biblica, Inc. Used by permission. All rights reserved worldwide.

Scripture references marked NKJV are from *The New King James Version*. ©1982, Thomas Nelson, Inc. Used by permission.

Scripture references marked NLT are from *The Holy Bible, New Living Translation*, ©1996, 2004. Used by permission of Tyndale House Publishers, Inc., Wheaton, Ill. 60189. All rights reserved.

All emphases in Scripture have been added by the author.

Hardcover ISBN: 978-1-4335-0778-6
PDF ISBN: 978-1-4335-0779-3
Mobipocket ISBN: 978-1-4335-0780-9
ePub ISBN: 978-1-4335-2375-5
BGEA ISBN: 978-1-59328-503-6

Library of Congress Cataloging-in-Publication Data
Tchividjian, Tullian.
   Jesus + nothing = everything / Tullian Tchividjian.
     p. cm.
   Includes bibliographical references (p.) and index.
   Includes bibliographical references (p.) and index.
   ISBN 978-1-4335-0778-6 (hc)
     1. Christian Life—Presbyterian authors. I. Title. II. Title: Jesus plus nothing equals everything.
BV4501.3/T394   2011
248.4—dc22   2011014870

Crossway is a publishing ministry of Good News Publishers.

To my Dad,
Stephan B. Tchividjian
(July 29, 1939–January 23, 2010)

Your agonizing fight for physical life in 2009
fueled my agonizing fight for spiritual life in 2009.
Thanks, Dad.
I'll see you on the other side.

CONTENTS

ACKNOWLEDGMENTS

I have a confession to make: I'm addicted to the gospel. It burns inside of me. And it seems to get hotter every day. I can't stop thinking about it, talking about it, writing about it, reading about it, wrestling with it, reveling in it, standing on it, and thanking God for it. For better or for worse, my focus has become myopic. My passion has become singular. Lesser things don't distract me as easily. I'm not as anxious as I used to be. I don't fret over things as much. I'm more relaxed. What others think of me (either good or bad) doesn't matter as much as it used to. I'm enjoying life more. The pressure's off. I'm beginning to understand the length and breadth of the freedom Jesus purchased for me. I'm beginning to realize that the gospel is way more radical, offensive, liberating, shocking, and counterintuitive than any of us realize. And that's beginning to be okay with me. Like Aslan in C. S. Lewis's *Chronicles of Narnia*, the gospel is good but not safe.

This book is a record of how I got to this point. It highlights the liberating life lessons, theological lessons, and biblical lessons God taught me during the most difficult year of my life—2009—the year God helped me rediscover the now-power of the gospel in the crucible of excruciating pain.

I didn't get here all by myself, though. I had a lot of help. There are tons of people who walked this road with me, carried me when I needed it, and stuck by my side when it would have been easier for them to walk away.

To my Coral Ridge Church family: I love you all so much.

Thank you for allowing me to be your pastor and for supporting me along the way. We went through the fire, but by God's grace we've come out on the other side. Keep your seatbelts fastened. The gospel revolution is just getting started.

To the elders, deacons, and staff at Coral Ridge: for over two years now, we have stood side by side and back to back. Thanks for your protection, counsel, support, love, and help. You are all dear friends, faithful followers of Jesus, and steel-spined soldiers of grace. It's an honor to serve with you.

To my gospel mentors: there are far too many to name them all. But ten in particular have sharpened my understanding of the gospel significantly over the last two years: Mike Horton, Steve Brown, Rod Rosenbladt, Gerhard Forde, Tim Keller, Paul Tripp, Elyse Fitzpatrick, Scotty Smith, Jerry Bridges, and Harold Senkbeil. I am extremely grateful to God for all of you and the way you have challenged and encouraged me through either your writing or your friendship or, in most cases both.

To my friends at Crossway: you have been interested in, and supportive of, this project from beginning to end. You are all a delight to work with!

To my editor Thomas Womack: once again you have helped me turn sermons into a book. Your skill is unmatched and your friendship undeserved.

To my children Gabe, Nate, and Genna: my ongoing prayer for you is that you will come to increasingly love and be liberated by God's unconditional, undeserved, uncontrollable grace. He loves you because he loves you. And so do I. No strings attached. Don't ever forget it!

And, finally, to my wife, Kim: you cried with me, bled with me, and never wavered. When we were in the wilderness and it seemed preferable to me to go back to Egypt, your steadiness helped me see the Promised Land and kept me marching onward with grit and determination. You are tough and tender, sweet and strong. You keep me grounded, focused, and accountable. You are always supportive of me but never impressed by me. A perfect combination. God knew exactly what he was doing when he brought you to me seventeen years ago. Apart from God's saving me, you are, hands down, the best thing that has ever happened to me. I love you, honey!

PART ONE

EVERYTHING

=

1

GOD'S MERCY
IN MY MISERY

===

Never had I experienced anything so tough. I could hardly eat, had trouble sleeping, and was continually battling nausea. I felt at the absolute end of myself.

God, what in the world are you doing?

I needed resurrecting.

It was the summer of '09, the low point in the most challenging and difficult year of my life. Thankfully, at the end of June, as we always did, my family and I left home to go on vacation for a couple of weeks. Never had I needed it more.

SO DIFFERENT

The contrast then with what my life had been like only twelve months earlier could hardly have been more stark. The year before, I had been pastoring New City Church, a thriving, five-year-old congregation I'd started just north of Fort Lauderdale, Florida. We had hundreds of people attending two morning services at New City every Sunday in our rented high school facility, and we sensed how much we were growing together in our commitment to serving the liberating power of the gospel to one another and our needy city. Understandably, we had plenty of confident expectations about our future together.

Just as understandably, another congregation a few miles south of us was facing its future with lots more questions, clouded with uncertainty. Coral Ridge Presbyterian in Fort Lauderdale was a church my family had attended for part of my childhood, when we first moved to South Florida in the 1970s. Founded a half-century ago by Dr. D. James Kennedy, Coral Ridge had become nationally known through its televised services (reaching as many as 3.5 million viewers weekly) and through Dr. Kennedy's widely followed Evangelism Explosion movement. The church's landmark worship facility—topped by a 300-foot spire and featuring a pipe organ with 6,600 pipes—had been dedicated by my grandfather Billy Graham, in February 1974 (I was nineteen months old). But by the twenty-first century, attendance there was in decline, and a further blow came with Dr. Kennedy's death in 2007.

Eventually, as Coral Ridge pursued its search for a successor to the only senior pastor the church had ever known, my name surfaced in the discussion. Over a period of several weeks, I was contacted a couple of times by people representing Coral Ridge's leadership, asking me to consider being one of the candidates for the position. That was honoring as well as mind-boggling. But after praying about it, and asking others to pray as well, I realized my interest level in pursuing it was zero. I knew I was already at the post where God had assigned me, and where he was doing a great work. I couldn't imaging stepping away.

As the months went by, a new and intriguing idea came into the picture. What if Coral Ridge and New City were to merge? Through some startling developments and conversations late in 2008, groups from each church began to sense that this idea had God's fingerprints all over it. Soon the elder teams of both churches were sensing that carefully exploring such a merger was the right thing before God for us all.

On a mid-January Sunday in 2009, both congregations heard

a public announcement about the potential merger, a plan that would install me as senior pastor of the new combined church. At the time, Fort Lauderdale's leading newspaper reported that the Coral Ridge congregation greeted the announcement with "gasps, then applause." But at New City, there were tears. I emphasized to them my conviction that God was asking us to put what we loved on the altar.

In the weeks ahead, there were plenty of people inside and outside both churches who wondered whether such a merger could ever really succeed. Even the Fort Lauderdale newspaper pointed out obvious contrasts, describing me as a pastor with a "scruffy face," "tan skin," and "a taste for surfing" and "mainstream music"—not exactly the image that a well-established church like Coral Ridge had developed over its five decades.

The newspaper quoted me as saying that Coral Ridge's willingness to consider the merger was a positive sign of their flexibility: "For anyone who thinks Coral Ridge can't make any changes, this unconventional move demonstrates that they can and are willing to."

Nevertheless, I had as many questions about it as anybody else.

"FASTEN YOUR SEATBELTS"

I had to admit that at New City I sometimes felt the desire to move faster, higher, and farther than we'd so far attained in our congregation. I had dreams and ambitions about what I wanted us to become. But a big part of me also wanted to see the door firmly closed to the possibility of any merger with Coral Ridge, especially given how widely the two congregations seemed to differ in culture and mind-set and expectations.

When I talked to my grandfather about it, he told me, "All this scares me, but I trust God to act."

And God *was* acting. I sensed clear indications that he was pushing this forward. So did the elder teams in both churches, who in March agreed unanimously on the merger plan that a joint team from both churches had drafted. That same month I preached for the first time at Coral Ridge, and this was followed by a congregational vote. More than 90 percent of the Coral Ridge congregation cast their ballots in support of the merger. On Easter Sunday, both congregations began meeting together for the first time. A month later, on May 10, 2009, I was formally installed as senior pastor of the combined church.

The next day I offered the congregation a written message, through my blog, entitled "Come Die with Me." I first recalled my impressions of the previous evening:

> As one new church, we celebrated God's promise to build his church. Through the praying, praising, preaching, and taking of vows, God came near and reminded us that it's all about him and his glory, his fame, his renown. God's presence was indeed thick and unmistakable.

I reviewed the main thrust of a sobering message given us that evening by my friend John Wood, a Presbyterian pastor from Tennessee:

> With God-fueled fire in his eyes, he reminded all of us that bearing fruit requires death. Jesus said we must die in order that we might live. Daily Christian living, in other words, is daily Christian dying: dying to our trivial comforts, soul-shrinking conveniences, arrogant preferences, and self-centered entitlements, and living for something much larger than what makes us comfortable and safe. *God does everything through people who understand they're nothing. And God does nothing through those who think they're everything.*

Then I built on John's point in expressing my expectation of God's great work in our future together at Coral Ridge. And I extended an invitation:

I believe this one new church will thrive beyond anything we could ever ask or imagine if it's packed with gospel-intoxicated people: people who understand that since Christ laid his life down for us, we must lay our lives down for others. . . . A gospel-saturated church is a church filled with people who give everything they have because they understand that *in Christ they already have everything they need.* . . .

So, having been duly installed and charged, I invite all of you to spend your life dying with me.

Let this one new church show the watching world what human life and community can look like when a pack of God-centered missionaries spend their life seeking to serve rather than be served.

My closing line: "Fasten your seatbelts."

All that—including the final admonition—were words I would need to urgently remember in the weeks and months ahead. Although I'd expected some tough times to crop up as two very different congregations merged into one, I had no idea how ugly and messy it would become.

CRESCENDO OF PAIN

With the merger and the leadership transition, a small but vocal group of long-time Coral Ridge members immediately began voicing opposition to practically any and every change we initiated or even considered at the church. Blogs were posted, notes and letters were circulated—some anonymously—with false accusations about me. Just three months after I arrived, a vigorous petition drive was started to get me removed, and it gained steam. Some people began lamenting the huge mistake they'd made in agreeing to the merger, and they grumbled that the whole thing had turned into a "hostile takeover." Their tone was frequently heated and vicious. Battle lines were drawn, rumors raced, and the spirits of those who supported me sagged. There was a crescendo of misunderstandings, frustration, and pain.

I continued in my determination to bring about what we believed were needed changes at the church, but the virulence of the opposition to them was almost more than I could bear. I was undergoing the shelling of my life—and I was plenty ready to quit and escape elsewhere. I was informed of possible other job offers from around the country, and believe me, they were tempting. It would have been so easy just to walk away from the turmoil I was in and never look back.

All that is what I was going through when, mercifully, vacation time rolled around in June 2009.

On our first morning away, I woke up still saturated with the misery that had been intensifying for so many weeks. I opened up my Bible; in the reading plan I was following, it so happened that the day's passages included the first chapter of Paul's letter to the Colossians.

As I read those verses—the glorious message of which we'll investigate together in the pages to come—my eyes were opened. God's Holy Spirit helped me see the incredible sufficiency of Christ and the gospel. I could see it with greater clarity and deeper personal application than I'd ever experienced. I sensed my miserable chains falling away.

My true situation came into focus. I'd never realized before how dependent I'd become on human approval and acceptance until so much of it was taken away in the roiling controversy at Coral Ridge. Before, in every church I'd been a part of, I was widely accepted and approved and appreciated. I'd always felt loved in church. Now, for the first time, I found myself in the uncomfortable position of being deeply disliked and distrusted, and by more than a few people. Now I realized just how much I'd been relying on something *other* than—something *more* than—the approval and acceptance and love that were already mine in Jesus.

IN FULL COLOR

In my misery I demanded an explanation from God. After all, I had done what he asked me to do—I had put "my baby" on the altar. And now this? Like Jonah in the belly of the great fish, I was arguing with God and making my case for why God owed me rescue. Worn out, afraid, and angry, I insisted that God give me my old life back. The gentle but straightforward answer from God that I received from the pages of Colossians that morning was simple but sobering: "It's not your old life you want back; it's your old idols you want back, and I love you too much to give them back to you."

I was being challenged by God to more fully understand exactly what I *already* had in Christ. For far longer than I recognized, I had been depending on the endorsement of others to validate me—to make me feel that I mattered.

God began rescuing me from that slavery by forcing me to rediscover the gospel.

I was learning the hard way that the gospel alone can free us from our addiction to being liked—that Jesus measured up for us so that we wouldn't have to live under the enslaving pressure of measuring up for others.

His good news met me in my dark place, at my deepest need. Through his liberating word, I was being transformed, freed, refreshed.

I started learning to see the many-faceted dimensions of the gospel in a more dazzling way. It's almost as if, for me, the gospel changed from something hazy and monochromatic to something richly multicolored, vivid, and vibrant. I was realizing in a fresh way the *now*-power of the gospel—that the gospel doesn't simply rescue us *from* the past and rescue us *for* the future; it also rescues us *in* the present from being enslaved to things like fear, insecurity, anger, self-reliance, bitterness, entitlement, and insignificance (more on all this later). Through my pain, I was being convinced all over again that the power of the gospel is just as necessary and relevant *after* you become a Christian as it is before.

In our new congregation, there would still be hardships ahead. In many ways, the worst struggles were still in front of us, weighing heavily on my heart, on my family's hearts, and on the hearts of so many in the church. But through those adversities, I would come to depend on God as never before. When that difficult year was over, I'd be able to look back and realize that *God seemed bigger to me than ever*, while I'd never been so small.

He had stripped me down—wrecked me afresh! And when he does that to a person—when you actually feel like you have *nothing*—Jesus becomes more to you than you ever could have hoped or imagined.

That June morning was when *Jesus plus nothing equals everything*—the gospel—became for me more than a theological passion, more than a cognitive catch-phrase. It became my functional lifeline. Rediscovering the gospel enabled me to see that:

> because Jesus was strong for me, I was free to be weak;
> because Jesus won for me, I was free to lose;
> because Jesus was someone, I was free to be no one;
> because Jesus was extraordinary, I was free to be ordinary;
> because Jesus succeeded for me, I was free to fail.

This began to define my life anew in bright and liberating ways.

I believe God wants this liberating truth to define your life as well, and also to define the life of the church.

So, together let's explore the liberating explosion of *Jesus plus nothing equals everything*.

2

WANTING IT ALL

The phrase on this book's cover just sounds right, doesn't it? There's a certain ring to it as the phrases build:

> Jesus . . .
> plus nothing . . .
> equals everything.

I'll even wager you've given those words a quick and appreciative nod. It's just not a statement you'd ever be much inclined to disagree with—on its surface, at least. But what does it *really* mean? Why should it merit any further thought, let alone intense scrutiny? How could it possibly help you and me?

It's a statement that's set up as an equation, of course, but what this expression leads to at the end is not so much a sum as an attainment, a destination, a realization—an *experience*. So, to analyze it more closely and understand it more fully, let's try starting at the end of it—with the "everything." That's where we'll focus in these opening pages; then we'll carefully work our way backward toward the statement's beginning. We'll see what we discover along the way. And then, with new and deeper insight (I hope and pray), we'll proceed through this proposition from front to back, further milking it for all its worth. So, topically speaking, here's this book's basic outline:

    a) Everything
    b) Nothing
    c) Jesus
        d) Jesus
        e) plus *Nothing*
        f) equals *Everything*

And now, fasten your seatbelts, because one thing I'm sure of: *Jesus plus nothing equals everything* is a truth that no one on earth grasps fully enough as yet. It's a profound reality just begging to be pried open so that we find amazingly more to love and enjoy about it.

EVERYTHING? REALLY?

Isn't it interesting how this implied promise of *everything* is not something we instinctively resist or shy away from. When you first saw this book's cover, I doubt you reacted to the title by thinking, "But who even wants or needs 'everything'? *Barely enough* is all I care about—and maybe even less. *The minimal life* is what I'm after; keep it stunted, keep it slight, keep it small. Limits, deficiency, constriction, confinement—hey, I'm good with all that."

No, that's not at all what you thought. Because the human soul insists otherwise. Throughout history, philosophers and sages couldn't help noticing the hole that's in our hearts, the universal and insatiable yearning to experience *more*, to attain something higher, deeper, fuller, richer, stronger, wiser, safer, happier. Deeply and sincerely, we want to live larger than we do, and with an epic, sweeping perspective. We crave a full acceptance and favor, we crave a lasting affection and approval, we crave meaning and purpose, and we crave a freedom from our limitations and restrictions and failures.

Whatever security, happiness, relief, rescue, affirmation,

meaning, and sense of purpose we're privileged enough to experience—it still isn't enough. Something within us hungers for what we don't yet have. And whether or not we realize it, this drives our every pursuit. We crave the more—sometimes wildly and illogically, it seems, but consistently, recurrently. We'll try anything and everything to fill this vacuum we abhor.

Observing this phenomenon, the wisest of the wise have concluded that it points to God. Augustine caught this perhaps most famously and succinctly, sixteen centuries ago, on the opening page of his *Confessions*, where he told the Lord, "You made us for yourself, and our hearts are restless until they rest in you." Was any better description of humanity ever written?

Are you experiencing any restlessness in your life somewhere? I am. I'm sure we all are, if we're honest. Because we crave the *everything*.

Twelve centuries after Augustine, the brilliant mind of Pascal took up this same human predicament. "All men seek happiness," he noted; "this is the motive of every action of every man, even of those who hang themselves." (So perceptive, that man Pascal.) He then went on to cite humanity's endless sighs and groans as confirmation that nobody ever really satisfies this innate desire: "All complain—princes and subjects, noblemen and commoners, old and young, strong and weak, learned and ignorant, healthy and sick, of all countries, all times, all ages, and all conditions." Such universal dissatisfaction ought to convince us "of our inability to reach the good by our own efforts," Pascal says, but it's a lesson we fail to grasp: "And thus, while the present never satisfies us, experience dupes us," and so onward we stumble "from misfortune to misfortune."

Although, Pascal continues, "there was once in man a true happiness," nothing remains of this—except "the mark and empty trace, which he in vain tries to fill from all his surroundings, seeking from things absent the help he does not obtain in things present. But these are all inadequate." Why are they all inadequate? Pascal reaches the astute deduction: "Because the infinite abyss can only be filled by an infinite and immutable object, that is to say, only by God Himself."[1]

The *everything* we crave is so vast, so comprehensive, so deep, so high, that it extends even this far—to *God himself.*

OUR DILEMMA

In our own day, Paul David Tripp—counselor, pastor, and author—takes his own turn at examining all this. In *A Shelter in the Time of Storm*, he tells his reader about "the dilemma of your humanity"; then, with wise and loving care, he shows where this can lead:

> You are clearly not in control of the details or destiny of your life, yet as a rational, purposeful, emotional being, you cry for a deep and abiding sense of well-being. In your quest, what you are actually discovering is that you were hardwired to be connected to Another. . . . In this way, every human being is on a quest for God; the problem is we don't know that, and in our quest for stability, we attempt to stand on an endless catalog of God-replacements that end up sinking with us. . . .
>
> There is a Rock to be found. There is an inner rest to be experienced that's deeper than conceptual understanding, human love, personal success, and the accumulation of possessions. There is a rock that will give you rest even when all of those things have been taken away. That rock is Christ, and you were hardwired to find what you are seeking in him. In his grace, he won't play hide-and-seek with you. In your weakness and weariness, cry out to him. He will find you, and he will be your Rock.
>
> He is the rock for which you are longing, he is the one who alone is able to give you the sense that all is well. And as you abandon your hope in the mirage rocks of this fallen world, and begin to hunger for the true rock, he will reach out, and place you on solid ground.[2]

I'm reminded at this point of the famous words of C. S. Lewis in *Mere Christianity:* "If I find in myself a desire which no experience in this world can satisfy"—and don't we all?— "the most probable explanation is that I was made for another world."[3] In Lewis's argument, that "world," of course, is eternal life in the presence of God our savior.

So, to summarize: Augustine says we're doomed to restlessness apart from God; Pascal sees an infinite abyss inside us that only God can fill; and we're all hard-wired for a quest after God, Tripp echoes. And all this is proven, Lewis argues, when our very own deepest desires go unfulfilled.

To get a scriptural focus on this built-in human hunger for everything, all it takes is a glance at a few Bible passages, though countless others would steer us in this direction as well.

Genesis 1 lays the strongest of foundations for man's link with *everythingness.* First and foremost is the fact of our being made in God's image, created after his likeness. That's a staggering truth, overflowing with richness and mystery. To be in some significant way *like God*—to actually represent him somehow, to in some way mirror him—what greater bond with vastness and greatness and momentous meaning could there possibly be than that?

Moreover, Genesis emphasizes that newly created man was assigned dominion "over *every* living thing that moves on the earth," while for food he had his choice of "*every* plant yielding seed that is on the face of all the earth, and *every* tree with seed in its fruit" (Gen. 1:28–29). Don't fail to appreciate the scope here. By divine design, man as originally created enjoyed a wide-horizon existence characterized chiefly not by limits but by the lack of them. His daily sphere was suffused with a very real sense of *everything.* And that everything included, most importantly, an unhindered relationship with God himself.

Flip over to the Bible's ending, and we see an unlimited

comprehensiveness emphasized again, this time for humanity's future existence—yours and mine. It encompasses the cosmos, and it's all fresh and new: "a new heaven and a new earth, for the first heaven and the first earth had passed away" (Rev. 21:1). The Lord on his throne declares, "Behold, I am making all things new" (v. 5). Once more, don't miss the massive scope here.

We don't forget that between Genesis 1 and the last pages of Revelation there unfolds an epic story marked by incalculable tragedies. But grasp again what God will do for his redeemed people in the end: "[He] will wipe away *every* tear from their eyes" (Rev. 7:17). Pause there for a moment. Can we even begin to appreciate what that statement embraces and what it makes possible in our experience? "And death shall be *no more*, neither shall there be mourning, nor crying, nor pain *anymore*, for the former things have passed away" (21:4).

MORE THAN TALK?

Yet Revelation 21 and 22 are future. For now, we can't quite get beyond the restlessness that Augustine relates, the abyss that Pascal observes, the quest for solid ground that Tripp writes of, and the unfulfilled desires Lewis mentions—all of it pointing Godward.

If those men are right, then there's an *everything*—a fullness, a completeness, a life-abundance—that is in fact available and attainable, and surely it's worth whatever effort to discover how to actually experience it.

But then, all around us our cynical, secular culture scoffs at all this we-so-desperately-need-God talk. To them, what Augustine and Pascal and the others speak of looks like self-flattering myth fulfillment—nothing more than quaint, sentimental nonsense.

"Oh no," modern religious minds will quickly counter. "It's true—*God and God alone* can really satisfy." For many or most of these religious folks, however, isn't that response mere talk? Isn't it just a parroted platitude, a concept assented to but never quite thoroughly embraced? Isn't it right that these people's religious lives can end up looking as empty as anyone's—falling far short of demonstrating the satisfaction they claim their God supplies?

And lots of them know it. Deep down, they're only too aware of this inconsistency, so painfully disappointing. So they let their souls sink into a sad and weary resignation. What's the use? Why expect more?

Eventually, they may even lose all faith in the only-God-can-satisfy claim. They lose their proper sense of the *everything.*

Yet deep down, the desires are still there, of course, intense as ever.

So what do we do with them?

PART TWO

NOTHING

+

3

STILL SEARCHING

=

Here's at least one way that I'd guess you and I are alike: I suspect that you (like me) have no real mental objection to the notion that God, all by himself, is plenty capable of providing all the "everything" we human beings could ever crave. A rational assumption about a big God is probably already stickered with a "fact" label and shelved neatly in the compartment within your brain (like the one in mine) where such truisms are sorted and stored.

So, to move forward in this discussion—if we want *Jesus plus nothing equals everything* to touch any real nerve—it will take a deeper engagement than that with our intellects alone. We'll need to delve into secret, shadowy regions of the heart. We'll have to risk a plunge into soul depths.

MORE RESTLESSNESS

Think again about Augustine's classic observation that our hearts are restless till they find rest in God. When I mentioned it earlier, I asked whether you recognize any restlessness in your own life. Perhaps you thought, "Some, I suppose," or "Not much," or even "No, not currently." But if you genuinely searched inside yourself more thoroughly, I think you wouldn't get far before finding significant restlessness. And the more deeply you investigated (if you're brave enough to do that), the more traces of it you'd probably find.

Whatever indications of restlessness you did discover, at whatever level, I believe the reason for its being there is this: we're trying to find our rest in something smaller than Jesus. And the more closely we examine those points of restlessness—the more light we shed on them—the quicker we realize, "On this particular issue, in this particular part of my life, I'm looking to something or someone smaller than Jesus to be for me what only Jesus can be."

BENEATH OUR ADDICTIONS

Occasionally I talk with people in counseling sessions where the issue is an addiction—pornography, gambling, workaholism, whatever. One of the questions I'll ask them is this: *What are you missing in life that prompts you to go after this particular addiction?* They're deciding to yield to that addiction, to give themselves to it, to embrace it, because something else they crave is lacking. Deep down they sense that something necessary, something enlivening, is missing.

They're using the addiction to try and fill the void.

So what's the *real* need they're seeking to fill? I urge them to first try figuring that out, at the heart level.

Fundamentally, somebody's worst addiction is no different from whatever issues of restlessness you and I face. And the first question to ask is always the same: What are we *really* after? Inside us, what truly needs to be there that isn't? It might be acceptance or approval, in various ways, from various people. It could be a sense of identity or direction or significance or purpose. It may well be the experience of security or of freedom and deliverance.

We're looking for all these things all the time.

Let me urge you to get unusually quiet and to simply ask yourself: *Where* exactly am I experiencing agitation, impatience, unease, anxiety? Why is it there? What's that really all about? Identify where your restlessness is rooted—because that's where a confrontation with the gospel is needed.

Later, I'll be asking you again to examine yourself like that—but first, let's spend time trying to better understand how to make the most of this kind of self-inspection.

WHERE WE FAIL TO LOOK

Ultimately, the void we seek to fill should *not* be there. It's good that we want to plug these gaping holes we're sensing. We're right in wanting to find and fill up what's missing.

But how will we go about doing that? How should we proceed?

Ideally, our best starting point is a recognition of this fact: whatever deficiency lies at the deepest root of our restlessness—no matter how big or small, whether it's life-gripping or comparatively trivial—the missing component is something very specific that *Christ has already secured for restless sinners like you and me.*

However, that's not where any of us ever look naturally to fill our need.

Obviously, before we were Christians, it was never our natural bent to seek all our satisfaction in Christ and the gospel; but even after God saves us, that isn't where we naturally turn.

In fact, when it comes to Christian life and experience, many of us have understood the gospel as the thing that *gets* us in, while the thing that then *keeps* us in (we assume) is our own effort and performance. We recognize that the gospel ignites the Christian life, but we often fail to see that it's also the fuel to keep us going and growing as Christians.

Unless we come to see and embrace the fact that the gospel never loses its importance in the practical outworking of the

Christian life, we'll continue to undercut and cheapen the gospel's impact.

ADDING ON

So if we aren't naturally prone to look to the finished work of Jesus for us as it's presented in the gospel for the "everything"— where *are* we looking?

Typically, it's not that Christians seek to blatantly replace the gospel. What we try to do is simply *add* to it.

You wonder, *Come on, can there really be much serious harm in that?* Yes, there can be, and there is.

Maybe you recall how this "addition" concept is brought out in C. S. Lewis's famous work *The Screwtape Letters*. As the high-ranking demon Screwtape trains his protégé Wormwood in satanic strategies against Christians, he discusses how (in Screwtape's words) "to keep them in the state of mind I call 'Christianity And.'" Screwtape gives a few examples (reflecting some fads from Lewis's time, the mid-twentieth century): "Christianity and the New Psychology, Christianity and the New Order, Christianity and Faith Healing," and even "Christianity and Vegetarianism."[1] These were all various manifestations of the urgent, Devil-fostered temptation believers face to *add something else* to our faith in Jesus and the gospel—all because of those deficiencies we sense in our own experience.

Today, Screwtape's list would doubtless look different. The currently tempting formulas might include "Christianity and coolness," "Christianity and self-affirmation," "Christianity and self-improvement," "Christianity and personal progress," or "Christianity and spiritual formation." There's a host of causes that might crop up: "Christianity and environmentalism," "Christianity and home schooling," "Christianity and social justice," "Christianity and diversity and tolerance," not to mention abundant "Christianity and political action" variations—liberal, conservative, libertarian, hope-and-change, take-back-America, whatever.

Besides those, there are plenty of extras that have timeless appeal for any and all generations: "Christianity and popularity," "Christianity and success," "Christianity and power," "Christianity and social status," "Christianity and reform," even "Christianity and tradition."

The list could go on and on. It will include whatever we're clinging to, whatever we won't let go of because we're using it to fill the void only God can fill.

Screwtape is telling the demon Wormwood that if he wants to distract Christians, if he wants to debilitate them, if he wants to keep them off course, powerless, and ineffective, simply make sure they never come to a place of believing that "mere Christianity" is enough. Make them feel good about affixing something further to the faith. It could be the latest fad; though perhaps far more likely it's a more personal fixation or obsession that grips us because of our endless, aching search to fill our inner hollowness.

Christianity and . . . For many of us, it may be Jesus and our achievements, Jesus and our strengths, Jesus and our reputation, Jesus and our relationships, Jesus and our family's prosperity, Jesus and our ambitions and goals and dreams, Jesus and our personal preferences and tastes and style, Jesus and our spiritual growth, Jesus and our hobbies and recreational pursuits and entertainment habits—and, especially, Jesus and our personal set of life rules.

Whatever it is our heart is drawn to—a cultural trend, a cause, a diversion, a personal "passion," a relationship, a pursuit, a venture, a comfortable routine—and however subtly it pulls us in, the cold, hard truth is that almost immediately *it becomes an idol*, and our heart grabs hold. As Martin Luther once said, "Whatever your heart clings to and confides in, that is really your God"—your functional savior.

Jesus plus X. The formula looks so innocent and harmless, even commendable (we're helping Jesus out!). But no such equation can ever lead anywhere good. Ultimately there can be only one equation—*Jesus plus nothing.* Anything we try to add to Christ ultimately results in what Michael Horton calls "Christless Christianity" (which he explains in a must-read book with that title).[2]

John Calvin famously said that all our hearts are idol-making factories. He understood how all of us are drawn down this idolatry track every day, Christian people and non-Christian people, in-church people and out-of-church people. We habitually look to something or someone smaller than Jesus for the things we crave and need. And none of it is ever large enough to fill the void.

IDOLATRY DEFINED

Idolatry is simply trying to build our identity on something besides God. An idol is anything that's usurping the proper place of God in our lives. An idol is anything or anyone that you conclude, in your heart, you *must* have in order for your life to be meaningful, valuable, secure, exciting, or free.

Here's one way to get your idols into focus: simply think about whatever it is in your life that, if you lost it, would make you want to quit living. Or, to put it positively, what are you *really* living for? What are you functionally depending on to make life worth living? Ultimately, if it's anything or anyone other than Jesus, then it's become an idol.

Most idols in themselves are good things, good gifts from God—our spouse, our children, our hopes and dreams, our work, our success, our skill, our looks, our reputation. The trouble comes when we transform these into *ultimate* things. We end up depending on these things and these people to provide us with the meaning and purpose and freedom and security and significance that only Jesus can provide.

I told you in chapter 1 how I'd never realized how dependent I'd become on human approval and acceptance until God took that away. In and of itself, human approval and acceptance are not bad things. They are, in fact, a gift from God. But I had turned them into idols by making them my primary source of meaning and value and worth and significance, so that without them I was miserable and depressed.

Like the pain I experienced, your pain right now could be God prying open your life and heart in order to remove a gift of his that you've been holding onto more dearly than him. Or, to put it into the form I once read from Paul Tripp: "How is your present disappointment, discouragement, or grief a window on what has *actually* captured your heart?"[3]

Jesus said he came to set the captives free. He came to liberate us from bondage. This explains why God is so passionate about smashing our idols.

So what *are* you trusting in, *other than Jesus*, to gain acceptance or approval, to experience security and significance, to find meaning and purpose, to discover identity and direction?

ALL NOTHINGNESS

I know you understand that this idolatry we're desperately endangered by isn't merely bowing down to some engraved wooden or stone statue, like in ancient times, or in some back-jungle heathen culture. And yet the biblical bottom line concerning that very form of false-god worship is the same as for our own sophisticated, twenty-first-century idolatry.

Here's that bottom line: God announces to all such idols, "Behold, you are *nothing,* and your work is *less than nothing*" (Isa.

41:24). He declares this about idols: "Behold, they are all a delusion" (41:29). They "do not profit" (44:9). "They are worthless" (Jer. 10:15).

The New Testament confirms it: "An idol has no real existence" (1 Cor. 8:4); idols are therefore "vain things" (Acts 14:15; "useless," NKJV; "worthless," NIV).

In all our lives, idolatry's accomplishment is only an absolute, abominable *nothingness*—the totally opposite effect of why we create and cherish and cling to those idols in the first place.

Jesus gives us a piercing picture of this nothingness at the end of Luke 16, in his famous account of the rich man and Lazarus. The story is well worth revisiting while we have the dynamics of idolatry in mind.

Interestingly, tradition down through the centuries has occasionally assigned a name to the rich man in this parable. The most prominent name is *Dives* (pronounced DI-veez), a Latin word for "wealthy man." A traditional English folk song about Dives and Lazarus goes back centuries and under that title has been preserved in later classical adaptations. But as Jesus told the parable, a pointed, ultimate fact about this guy is that *he has no name*. He built his identity around his wealth, around his pleasurable existence and luxurious possessions and sumptuous well-being—and lost it all at his death.

Meanwhile, in stark contrast in the story is an impoverished man whose name, Lazarus, Jesus immediately notes. In his earthly existence, Lazarus sat as a hungry beggar at the rich man's gate while dogs licked the sores covering his body. But, in eternity, Lazarus is carried by angels to be comforted at Father Abraham's side while the anonymous rich man is placed far across "a great chasm," where he suffers in flaming anguish in a place of "torment." When he calls out in agony, begging for mercy, Father Abraham addresses him not by name, but simply as "child" (v. 25). Having anchored his identity in his material pursuits, his accomplishments, and his stuff—having made them his idols—this man consequently forfeited his very identity. He literally lost himself!

All idolatry heads us down this path to no-nameness. And Jesus's story reminds us that far from being some vague, painless, amorphous existence, that ultimate condition of nothingness is acutely painful in every way. Inwardly and outwardly, it brings anguish and torment. That's the tragic destiny Jesus wants us to connect with idolatry in our understanding of it.

WHAT'S MISSING?

So let me ask you once more, as you get quiet and still: Deep within you, where is that restlessness, that agitation, that impatience, that anxiety? Why is it there? What is it you're missing, and you're trying to fill the gap?

4

BLACK HOLES

═

These idols we're tempted to turn to, these agents of nameless nothingness, are everywhere. "There are more idols in the world than there are realities," wrote Friedrich Nietzsche in *Twilight of the Idols*. This is true not only outside the church but also within it.

In fact, according to the Bible, the greatest threat to the gospel's advance in this world, and the greatest threat to gospel growth in your life and in mine, is a particular strain of idolatry that arises not from outside the church but from inside. It's a big part of why we're told, "It is time for judgment to begin at the household of God" (1 Pet. 4:17).

And what is this huge threat?

THE GREATEST THREAT

The Bible makes it clear that the gospel's premier enemy is the one we often call "legalism." I like to call it *performancism*. Still another way of viewing it, especially in its most common manifestation in Christians, is *moralism*. Strictly speaking, those three terms—legalism, performancism, and moralism—aren't precisely identical in what they refer to. But there's so much overlap and interconnection between them that we'll basically look at them here as one thing.

And what really is that one thing?

Well, it shows up when we fail to believe the gospel. It shows up when behavioral obligations are divorced from gospel declarations, when imperatives are disconnected from gospel indicatives. Legalism happens when *what we need to do*, not what Jesus has already done, becomes the end game.

Our performancism leads to pride when we succeed and to despair when we fail. But ultimately it leads to slavery either way, because it becomes all about *us* and what we must do to establish our own identity instead of resting in Jesus and what he accomplished to establish it for us. In all its forms, this wrong focus is anti-gospel and therefore enslaving.

It is typically displayed in someone who's trying to keep his or her preferred list of religious rules. At root, what this person tries to accomplish is really no different from what the secular person attempts by deliberately breaking those same rules. Both see *what they do* as the means to obtain what they're so desperately hungering for deep within. Both look to self to satisfy what only God can satisfy. For both, *it all depends on them,* not on Christ. As A. W. Pink once wrote, "The great mistake made by people is hoping to discover in themselves that which is to be found in Christ alone."[1]

Both are running away from Jesus, not toward him. Both are ignoring Jesus, not submitting to him. Both are self-rescue projects—both are endeavoring to save, sanctify, and satisfy themselves on their own terms and by their own power. Some pursue this by trying to break free of constraints, while others do it by multiplying constraints of their own choosing. And because of the versatile craftiness of the human heart, a good many people try their own unique and intricate blending of *both* these approaches.

Accepting the reality of this basic tendency in us all can be very difficult, especially for those of us who've been in church a long time. We know it's wrong to worship immorality, like everybody out in the world seems to be doing; we find it harder to see that it's just as wrong to worship morality, like everybody in the church seems to be doing.

In our bones, we know that God hates unrighteous "bad" works; we're not nearly so convinced that he hates self-righteous "good" works just as much, if not more. In fact, the most dangerous thing that can happen to you is that you become proud of your obedience.

In his excellent book *A More Radical Gospel*, the late Lutheran theologian Gerhard Forde writes:

> Our misdeeds are not the real root of the problem. They are just what the tradition called actual sins. There is a much more serious problem, what the tradition called original sin. It is much more subtle and inevitably hidden from us. The relationship is broken by the presumption of our ethical behavior, our morality, our good deeds, our insistence on doing it ourselves. The relation is broken because these too turn us quite simply against grace. . . . The Almighty God desires simply to be known as the giver of the gift of absolute grace. To this we say "no." We say, rather, that we intend to make it on our own, that grace is "too cheap." Then the relationship is destroyed just as surely as it was by our immorality.[2]

Our "good works" can become the very thing that gives us so much self-comfort and self-approval, this very thing we find so killingly attractive. Self-righteousness is our attempt to provide our own righteousness apart from his. God *hates* it because he loves us. And self-righteousness can lead only to the robbery of freedom.

WE CAN DO THIS

Why then are we so drawn to this legalism, this *performancism*, this self-morality quest?

Because it's another way we stroke our egos; it's another way we worship the idol of self. It's another way to remain independent and to "do it ourselves." Responding to our deep needs for acceptance and meaning and significance, we arrogantly assume that *we have the capacity* to somehow figure out and satisfy these needs on our own. We proudly put together our own ethical code, our own set of regulations and requirements, our own achievable standards and *obeyable* rules, all for ensuring the inner fulfillment our souls demand. We latch on to Bible verses that support our set of rules, and we justify our legalism under the guise of keeping the moral law as we perceive it in Scripture.

These self-imposed strictures that we devote ourselves to *seem* so right, so smart. (The apostle Paul would agree; all these things "have indeed an appearance of wisdom," Col. 2:23.) They promise safety and order and consistency in a world that's broken, chaotic, crazy, capricious—a world that frightens us. We hate unpredictability; we hate things being out of control. So we love rules because we think they'll protect us from all that. We're control freaks—filled with fear and slow to trust anyone outside ourselves.

Our rules become our substitute savior, and keeping those rules becomes our self-salvation project, with Jesus safely outside the picture. With enough rules and regulations set up, *we don't need Jesus.* After all, Jesus scares us—he's so unpredictable, so uncontrollable. Jesus's operating system—unconditional grace—is wild. It's unmanageable, uncontainable. It unsettles everything by wrestling control out of our hands, thereby putting us at the mercy of God. So we spend our lives trying to manufacture an existence that we can control.

All this happens inside us with the finest subtlety. In fact, most of us convince ourselves that we're actually *honoring* Jesus with our rules and regulations, that we're paying attention to him and pleasing him more than ever. But all the while, we're only demonstrating that we believe in ourselves much more than we do in Jesus. Our default faith mode is to trust, above all things, our own ability to create a safe, controllable, predictable world.

Legalism preserves our illusion that *we can do this*. On our own, we can generate the meaning and purpose and protection and significance we crave—a craving which will crush us if it isn't satisfied. *We can do it*—all it takes is doing the right things in the right way at the right time. Work hard enough at it, and all we deeply desire will be ours. And we'll congratulate ourselves, knowing we've achieved this without the help of others and without the help of God.

PREACH IT!

To make this situation even worse, our idolatrous self-focus is only intensified by what is typically taught and preached in our churches.

The fact is, a lot of preaching these days has been unwittingly, unconsciously seduced by moralism. Moralistic preaching only reinforces our inner assumption that our performance for God will impress him to the point of blessing us. A Christian may not struggle with believing that our good behavior is required to initially *earn* God's favor; but I haven't met one Christian who doesn't struggle daily with believing—somehow, someway— that our good behavior is required to *keep* God's favor.

So many contemporary sermons strengthen this slavery to self. "Do more, try harder" is the constant refrain. "Here is what you need to do; you're not doing it, so get out there and do it." Many sermons today provide nothing more than a "to do" list, strengthening our bondage to a performance-driven approach to the Christian life. It's all law (what we must do) and no gospel (what Jesus has done).

The world insists that the bigger we get and the better we feel about ourselves, the freer we become. Absorbing this narcissistic assumption, the modern church is all too often guilty of producing worship services that are little more than motivational, self-help seminars filled with "you can do it" songs and sermons. But what we find in the gospel is just the opposite. The gospel is good news for losers, not winners. It's for those who long to be freed from the slavery of believing that all of their significance, meaning, purpose, and security depend on their ability to "become a better you."

Moralistic preaching is stimulated by a fear of the scandalous freedom that gospel grace promotes and promises. The perceived fear is this: if we think too much and talk too much about grace and the radical freedom it brings, we'll go off the deep end with it. We'll abuse it. So to balance things out, we need to throw some law in there, to help make sure Christian people walk the straight and narrow.

It's part of a common misunderstanding in today's church, which says there are two equal dangers Christians must avoid. On one side of the road is a ditch called "legalism"; on the other is a ditch called "license" or "lawlessness." Legalism, they say, happens when you focus too much on law, on rules. Lawlessness, they say, happens when you focus too much on grace. Therefore, in order to maintain spiritual equilibrium, you have to balance law and grace. If you start getting too much law, you need to balance it with grace. If you start getting too much grace, you need to balance it with law. This dichotomy exposes our failure to understand gospel grace as it really is; it betrays our blindness to all the radical depth and beauty of grace.

I believe it's more theologically accurate to say that there is one primary enemy of the gospel—legalism—but it comes in two forms. Some people avoid the gospel and try to "save" themselves by keeping the rules, doing what they're told, maintaining the standards, and so on (I call this "front-door legalism"). Other people avoid the gospel and try to "save" themselves by breaking the rules, doing whatever they want, developing their own autonomous standards, and so on ("back-door legalism").

In other words, there are two "laws" we can choose to live by apart from Christ: the law that says, "I can find freedom and fullness of life if I keep the rules," and the law that says, "I can find freedom and fullness of life if I break the rules." Either way, you're trying to "save" yourself, which means both are legalistic because both are self-salvation projects.

So what some call "license" is just another form of legalism. People outside the church are typically guilty of break-the-rules legalism, while many inside the church are guilty of keep-the-rules legalism.

The biggest lie about grace that Satan wants the church to buy is the idea that it's dangerous and therefore needs to be kept in check. By believing that lie, we not only prove we don't understand grace, but we violate gospel advancement in our lives and in the church by perpetuating our own slavery. The truth is, disobedience happens not when we think *too much* of grace, but when we think *too little* of it.

As a pastor, one of my responsibilities is to disciple people into a deeper understanding of obedience—teaching them to say no to the things God hates and yes to the things God loves. All too often I've wrongly concluded that the only way to keep licentious people in line is to give them more rules—to lay down the law. The fact is, however, the only way licentious people start to obey is when they get a taste of God's radical, unconditional acceptance of sinners. Grace alone melts hearts and changes us from the inside out. Progress in obedience happens only when our hearts realize that God's love for us does not depend on our progress in obedience.

A "yes, grace—but" disposition is the kind of fearful posture that keeps moralism swirling around in our hearts and in the church. Subtly, the force of that falsehood gets transferred into sermons in which the driving dynamic is to get Christians behaving properly. Those messages appeal to our self-centered hearts, which are proudly pleased to latch onto such teaching.

ALL TOGETHER

Hearing those sermons, we breathe a sigh of relief, reinforced in our self-dependent quest for safety and control. For in our most delusional moments, we actually assume we're already there. *I have it all together*, we tell ourselves.

But none of us really has it together—*ever*. When we open our eyes, we'll see the Bible's confirmation that we're a lot worse off than we think we are—much more self-centered, arrogant, and greedy than we would ever admit to ourselves, let alone to other people. Those ingredients produce the most fertile breeding ground imaginable for self-idolatrous, legalistic moralism. And so it thrives.

That's a true picture of me, and that's you too. This stuff flourishes within us all. We're all guilty of it at some level. We're all guilty of adding to Jesus something of our own making, whatever that is. In fact, I'm just as guilty of it as you or anyone. I'm an expert on it.

HERE'S WHAT IT DOES

But for me as well as for you, the results of our legalistic, moralistic performancism are only tragic.

One thing it does is breed a sense of entitlement that turns us into complainers. We can see this in the famous parable Jesus told about the prodigal son. Sheer ugliness erupts in the older brother's attitude after he learns of the grace his father is lavishly bestowing on the prodigal. "Look," the elder son reproached his father, "these many years I have served you, and I never disobeyed your command, yet you never gave me a young goat, that I might celebrate with my friends. But when this son of yours came, who has devoured your property with prostitutes, you killed the fattened calf for him!" (Luke 15:29–30). He's telling him, *You owe me!* Which is exactly what we tell God (or at least we think it).

That's what legalism does to our relationship with our full-loving, grace-lavishing heavenly Father. We believe that if we *do, do, do* for him, he's *obligated* to do for us. And if he doesn't meet our expectations in this, we fuss and fume, at least inwardly. We totally forget Philippians 2:14: "Do all things without grumbling or questioning." In such moments we are in fact miles away from being able to genuinely obey that command.

The truth is, I'm a chronic complainer, and so are you. We're all complainers at some level, because we all live with a sense of entitlement at some level. And that kind of legalism makes us cantankerous.

A second tragic result of legalistic moralism is that it obscures the goodness of the good news. To reach people in our day, the gospel will have to be distinguished from moralism, because moralism is what most people outside the church think Christianity is all about—rules and standards and behavior and cleaning yourself up. Millions of people, both inside and outside the church, believe that the essential message of Christianity is, "If you behave, then you belong." From a human standpoint, that's why most people reject Christianity. A friend of mine told me the other day that the reason his now-deceased father never went to church was that he didn't think he was good enough. He said his dad thought church was all about a good person telling other good people how to be better people. But that's not what the Bible says.

My friends at Mars Hill Church in Seattle put together a quick list entitled "How to Become a Legalist," adapted from a sermon preached there by Mark Driscoll. Here's the procedure:

1) Make rules outside the Bible.
2) Push yourself to try and keep your rules.
3) Castigate yourself when you don't keep your rules.
4) Become proud when you do keep your rules.
5) Appoint yourself as judge over other people.
6) Get angry with people who break your rules or have different rules.
7) "Beat" the losers.[3]

Outsiders quickly detect this kind of self-righteous moralistic game that so many people inside the church are playing. They see how proud and self-righteous and flat-out unattractive these people become, and they want no part of it. People I've met who are turned off to Christianity will most often say it's because of the self-righteousness of professing Christians.

A third calamity from legalism is the way it traps us in slavery and despair. To define ourselves by what we must do, what we must accomplish, and who we must become—that's the epitome of slavery. When we believe, deep down, that God's blessing depends on how well we're behaving, we wither and groan under the heavy burden of self-reliance.

In this performancism, we eventually figure out that being the star of our own show actually makes life a tragedy. When life is all about *us*—what we can do, how we perform—our world becomes small and smothering; we shrink. To have everything riding on *ourselves* leads to despair, not deliverance.

When we're living by this legalism—trusting in our rule-keeping, our abilities, our performance—to sustain our little safe and self-controllable world that we're addicted to, someday it will all start to crumble. Our kids will spin out of control, or our marriage will, or our finances, or our career. And it's devastating. We've tried so hard to hide our frailty and weaknesses, building our self-esteem on our success at that, then suddenly those faults can't be hidden any longer. We feel hopeless.

The bitter truth slams us: those attractive idols we keep trustfully turning to are indeed "nothing" and "less than nothing" (Isa. 41:24). They're only black holes, the blackest of holes, dragging us down into desolation.

LOOK AGAIN

So I urge you once more: examine yourself. Dissect your heart. Recognize reality. What are you looking to (instead of Jesus) for meaning in life, for purpose, significance, security, direction, acceptance, approval? Ask yourself the same bold and probing question that Leo Tolstoy famously asked: "Is there any meaning in my life that the inevitable death awaiting me does not destroy?"[4] What are you living for? What are you depending on to provide the freedom, worth, and value that you crave?

The heart of the human problem is the problem of the human heart. Therefore rules, regulations, good behavior, personal success, and performance are never the solution. Behavior modification cannot change the human heart. Outside cleanup never leads to inside cleanup. Only inside cleanup leads to outside cleanup—and there's only One who can do that.

That's what I started seeing as never before back in the summer of '09.

PART THREE

JESUS

+

5

JESUS, ALL AND MORE

≡

Yes, our internal, transcendent longings are real and deep; in some ways, they often seem fathomless. Surely we ought to be able to do *something* about them.

But all the self-generated ways in which we strive to satisfy those yearnings, all the multitude of idols we set up and cling to, will always prove their nothingness in the end. They're *small*— ridiculously small—a fact which becomes utterly clear when our eyes are opened and we see just who alone is able to fill those gaping fissures in our soul.

In my super-stressful year of 2009, as I began the family vacation I've told you about, it was in Colossians that my soul reconnected with the supremacy and sufficiency of Christ. I discovered anew that the book of Colossians proclaims the pre-eminence of Jesus with as much richness and depth as anything we find in Scripture.

I returned often to that book in the days and weeks and months that followed, seeing and savoring it with new eyes and a new appetite. As I made my way through this epistle, and as I read seemingly every book written on Colossians to broaden and deepen my understanding of it, I was wrecked afresh. I was wrestled out of my comfort zone, pressed beyond where I feel secure. Its message was uncomfortably challenging, as the Great Physician wielded his scalpel.

I learned much more of what it means for us to be God-centered, gospel-saturated people. I learned just how enslaved I was to lesser things and how Jesus had come to set me free. I saw with clearer eyes that because I'm a sinner—because we're all sinners—God has to do a lot of chiseling and cutting and sanding in your life and mine as he increasingly centers our hearts more tightly on himself and the gospel.

No matter how young or old we are, he has work to do in our lives—he's still in the business of lovingly setting captives free.

COMPETING FORCES

When the apostle Paul wrote this letter to the Colossians (around AD 60), Colossae was a trade center with lots of travelers coming and going. It was a pluralistic place, a city where competing ideas and philosophies and worldviews got talked about and promoted, all maneuvering for recognition and supremacy. (Sound like any place or culture you're familiar with?)

Into that mix a church was planted, but the believers there found themselves frequently distracted by the forces and concepts vying for cultural allegiance.

Meanwhile, false teachers had arisen among the Colossian believers, tempting them with the promise of a deeper salvation, a better rescue, an enhanced freedom, a more enlightened knowledge, a heightened power in their lives that went beyond what Christ had done for them. These enticing influencers were pointing people away from Jesus and toward an appealing array of supplementary sources of blessing.

The world today isn't that much different, is it? All around us, we too are being sold a bill of goods; all around we're being bombarded with this idea that Jesus isn't enough.

Paul knew that this diminishing of Christ, this depreciation of God's Son, was the most dangerous and destructive heresy the

Colossian believers could possibly encounter. So he wrote them this epistle to show the superiority of Christ over all human philosophies and traditions, all human opinions and preferences and personalities and accomplishments. It was a superiority so overwhelming, so vastly devastating, so infinite, that we can hold fast unreservedly to this conclusion: *Jesus plus nothing equals everything—and everything minus Jesus equals nothing.*

A MEANINGFUL STRUCTURE

Like Paul's other letters, the epistle to the Colossians starts with *doctrinal* content (chapters 1 and 2), then transitions into the practical outworking of that doctrine (chapters 3 and 4). To use grammatical terms, Paul begins with the *vertical indicative* (what God in Christ has done for us), followed by the *horizontal imperative* (how we're to live in light of what God has done for us).

This order in Paul's teaching is vitally important. (The Bible is so rich and deep and multifaceted that we learn not simply from *what* the Bible says, but even from *how* the Bible says things.) Paul knew that the right way for us to think about our Christian lives is always to start with the vertical, then move to the horizontal. We're always to soak first in what God has already *done* before we set out to *do*. This intentional order is crucial because it distinguishes the gospel from moralism in our minds and helps us preserve the gospel from moralism in our actions.

Is Paul against morality? Of course not! His letters overflow with guidance and directives on how Christians should live. *Morality* is a good thing; on the other hand, moralism (as we've already discovered) is bad. When you affix an -*ism* to the end of a word, it generally recasts that idea into something ultimate and definitive, something to be supremely devoted to. So while the basic concept of morality is good, the extremity of moralism is not.

Paul was originally a Pharisee, and the Pharisees in the New Testament were the ultimate moralists. They were remarkably astute at making sure their external behavior was spic-and-span. Jesus, in fact, called them whitewashed tombs, acknowledging how outwardly "clean" they appeared. Everybody saw them as super-spiritual, the truly religious. "But on the inside," Jesus was telling them, "you're rotting and dead."

Moralism beats this drum: *If I improve, then I'll be accepted— by God, by others, even by myself.* But the gospel says something radically different. The gospel announces that everyone "in Christ" is already accepted by God because of Jesus's work for them. Therefore, no improvement, good behavior, or performance is necessary in order to experience the deep acceptance we long for and in fact strive for on a daily basis. This may seem like an impractical distinction, but it makes all the difference in the world.

So Paul does us a favor here by structuring Colossians (and his other letters) in such a way as to emphasize first what God has done for us in Christ, and only then explaining what our life and behavior should therefore become.

ULTRA DIMENSIONS

Paul doesn't teach doctrines in Colossians that we can't also find in his other letters. What's special about Colossians is not its doctrine; what's special about it is its *dimensions*. Paul's statements in Colossians about Christ are truly colossal—sweeping and immense, soaring beyond the boundaries of our understanding.

As we'll see, this letter also has huge things to say about our sin and even larger things to say about the gospel and what it accomplishes. In Colossians, Paul is writing to show that Jesus is big, our sin is big, the gospel is big, God's grace is big, and our rescue is big. There's nothing small at all about the truths this book communicates. And the epitome, the crowning point of all this vastness, is the incalculable greatness of Jesus Christ himself.

A NECESSARY MAGNITUDE

This magnitude of Christ Jesus is something we desperately need to understand better.

We need it because seeing him for all that he is will ultimately be the only way we can overcome our temptations to idolatry. In *Desiring God*, John Piper writes, "I know of no other way to triumph over sin long-term than . . . to gain a distaste for it because of a superior satisfaction in God."[1] And nothing can give us that "superior satisfaction in God" better than a clearer focus on Jesus and his greatness. When we're captured and captivated by who Jesus is, we'll be empowered and equipped to resist the constant temptations to settle for anything less.

And let me emphasize here that this more intense gaze at Christ is not just some intellectual effort but a matter of the heart's fascination, something thrilling and glad. Ultimately, it takes this kind of joy to defeat idolatry and sin. As the eighteenth-century Puritan Matthew Henry wrote, "The joy of the Lord will arm us against the assaults of our spiritual enemies and put our mouths out of taste for those pleasures with which the tempter baits his hooks."[2]

A SONG OF CHRIST'S SUPREMACY

The Colossians passage where the magnitude of Christ comes through most powerfully is verses 15–20 in chapter 1. Scholars say these lines may well have been originally a hymn to Christ. Paul breaks out here in songful praise, showing just how immense Jesus is, how mighty to save. One commentator observes that Paul seems almost to be in a state of controlled ecstasy here, awestruck by our Savior's vastness.

Even in a passage so brief, notice how often Paul keeps bringing up the *allness*, the *everythingness* that's connected with Jesus Christ:

> He is . . . the firstborn of all creation. For by him all things were created . . . all things were created through him and for him. And he is before all things, and in him all things hold together. . . . He is the beginning . . . that in everything he might be preeminent. For in him all the fullness of God was pleased to dwell, and through him to reconcile to himself all things. (Col. 1:15–20)

Paul is making giant declarations about the unqualified totality of Christ's preeminence. He wants his readers to be swept away by the sheer size of Christ, to savor his infinite supremacy and beauty and brilliance and power and trustworthiness.

The fact is, Jesus *owns* the concept of "everything." Paul wants us to be radically impressed by all that Jesus is—and to sense the truth that anything else in our lives must seem remarkably minor by comparison. God wants us to be awestruck by Christ's greatness, then strangely liberated by a fresh realization of our own smallness.

CREATION'S LORD

As Paul sings in these verses about the totality of Christ's superiority and magnificence, he highlights especially that Christ is sovereign and supreme over all creation (vv. 15–17) as well as over his church, his new creation (vv. 18–20).

In declaring that there's nothing in the created order bigger or more significant than Jesus, Paul speaks of Christ as "the first-born of all creation" (v. 15). This can't mean that Jesus himself is a created being, for that would contradict other Scriptures, including verses 16–17 right here in Colossians 1, where we see that all the created order was formed by, through, and for Christ.

"In the sharpest manner," the context here "distinguishes Christ from creation."[3]

So what Paul actually means by "the firstborn of all creation" is Christ's exalted status as being of first importance, of first rank, with every right and privilege over all creation. It's another way of saying that Jesus is God. Christ is *Lord* over creation.

I'm reminded of a famous saying from Abraham Kuyper, a Dutch theologian of a century ago: "There is not one square inch in all of God's creation that Jesus does not cry out, 'Mine!'" That's precisely what Paul is saying here.

The crescendo continues in Paul's song of Christ as he says, "In him all things hold together." In a mysterious way, Christ is the center adhesive of all creation.

This is true not just physically, but in every other way as well. That's why our being separated from Christ in any degree leads to breakdown and fragmentation in our lives. Are things falling apart in your life? Only Christ can bring your life back together in true wholeness.

THE CHURCH'S LORD

Paul goes on to say that as Christ is Lord over all creation, so also is he Lord over the church, as "the head of the body" (v. 18). Christ is the King of kings, the Lord of lords.

As Paul proclaims Christ's supremacy over the church, he again uses the term "firstborn"—Christ is "the beginning, the firstborn from the dead" (v. 18). In his ministry, Jesus had raised Lazarus and others from the dead, but Lazarus and the others would later die. Christ's own resurrection was the first of its kind, and one that all his followers will themselves experience as one day we're fully redeemed and transfigured.

The central significance of Christ's resurrection lies in the fact that's it's just the beginning of the saving, renewing, and resurrecting work of God that will have its climax in the resurrection of all believers and the restoration of the entire cosmos.

SEEING GOD IN CHRIST, AND CHRIST IN GOD

The crescendo swells incomparably higher as Paul writes, "In him all the fullness of God was pleased to dwell" (v. 19). The implications of those words are staggering, endlessly significant, infinite in depth and weight. We're meant to linger long on this statement, to keep unfolding its truth, because we'll never exhaust what it holds and what it means and all that it offers. It's worth all the attention we could ever give it.

It means, for example, that everything we read in Scripture about God the Father's goodness and greatness and gloriousness and holiness and righteousness is equally applicable to Christ, the Son of God. This is a fundamental reason for always reading the Old Testament with Jesus Christ in mind, since the picture of God we behold there is also the picture of Christ we're to have.

For example, think about the praises in the sampling of verses below—all true of Jesus, all descriptive of the magnitude of the glory of Christ, which is the fullness of God himself. You can use them freely, with a glad and grateful heart, to worship the Lamb of God in the kind of intimate fellowship with him you were created for.

> In your presence there is fullness of joy;
>   at your right hand are pleasures forevermore. (Ps. 16:11)

> The earth, O LORD, is full of your steadfast love. (Ps.119:64)

> For you are great and do wondrous things;
>   you alone are God. (Ps. 86:10)

Your righteousness, O God,
        reaches the high heavens.
You who have done great things,
        O God, who is like you? (Ps. 71:19)

Great is your mercy, O Lord. (Ps. 119:156)

All things are your servants. (Ps. 119:91)

Great is the LORD, and greatly to be praised,
        and his greatness is unsearchable. (Ps. 145:3)

Great is our LORD, and abundant in power;
        his understanding is beyond measure. (Ps. 147:5)

For how great is his goodness, and how great his beauty!
(Zech. 9:17)

The steadfast love of the LORD never ceases;
his mercies never come to an end. (Lam. 3:22)

This greatness of God in the person of Christ is why Paul can say
that "all the promises of God find their Yes in him"—in Christ
(2 Cor. 1:20).

EVERY BLESSING

So, Paul says, in Christ Jesus we encounter *all the fullness of God.*
This lofty phrase has also been rendered as "God in all his fullness," "all that God is," "the full nature of God," "the complete
being of God, "the totality of divine powers and attributes."[4]
Eugene Peterson's translation says that Christ is "so spacious . . .
so roomy, that everything of God finds its proper place in him
without crowding" (Col. 1:19 MESSAGE).

All of God is in Christ, and notice that Paul says it's all there
according to "the Father's good pleasure" (v. 19 NASB). The message Jesus heard from on high at his baptism in the Jordan River

is the one he has always heard, and hears forever: "You are my beloved Son; with you *I am well pleased*" (Luke 3:22).

And all of this is a blessing for you and me.

We can think of it as "a fullness of righteousness, wisdom, power, and every blessing," as John Calvin expresses it. "We must draw from the fullness of Christ everything good that we desire for our salvation," he says, "because such is the determination of God." Calvin continues, "Christ is all things to us; apart from him we have nothing."[5] Consequently, we rob ourselves of the freedom Christ secured for us whenever we embrace smaller things, substitute saviors, false gods—idols!

For Christians, Christ's fullness means *everything* for *everyone*. As the apostle John expressed it in introducing us to Christ in his Gospel, "From his *fullness* we have *all* received, grace upon grace" (John 1:16).

SEEING THE UNSEEABLE

In him all the fullness of God was pleased to dwell—these glorious words in Paul's praise song to Christ in Colossians point back to the song's opening phrase: "He is the image of the invisible God" (Col. 1:15). In Christ we can see what is otherwise unseeable— "God in himself . . . in his naked majesty," as Calvin puts it.[6]

What we get to see is incomparably dazzling and brilliant. We behold "the light of the gospel of the glory of Christ, who is the image of God," as Paul expresses it elsewhere (2 Cor. 4:4). This "image of God" is something "Christ always has been, is, and always will be"[7]—it's a solid "forever" truth, not some airy, abstract concept but a practical reality always available for our blessing and benefit.

This "image" phrasing lets us know that Jesus is God's exact likeness as well as the fully accurate manifestation or revelation of God. When we look at Christ in the New Testament (as well as in the Old), we never have to give ourselves a cautious mental check and think, *Oh, but that's Jesus, not God.* Seeing Jesus, we see God; and every glimpse of him is for our own constant enlightenment and encouragement, a light for our daily path: "For God, who said, 'Let light shine out of darkness,' has shone in our hearts to give the light of the knowledge of the glory of God in the face of Jesus Christ" (2 Cor. 4:6).

EVERYTHING, EVERYWHERE

As our eyes are opened in the Scriptures, our perception of Christ's fullness keeps expanding in every direction, enhancing everything we see and learn and know about him.

We recognize afresh that the church "is his body, the fullness of him who fills all in all" (Eph. 1:23).

We learn that the risen and glorified Christ is "the one who . . . ascended far above all the heavens, that he might fill all things" (Eph. 4:10).

We see how God has "appointed" Jesus "the heir of all things, through whom also he created the world" (Heb. 1:2).

And finally, on the Bible's last page, we hear the divine fullness resounding in the Savior's voice as he shouts, "I am the Alpha and the Omega, the first and the last, the beginning and the end" (Rev. 22:13).

This divine fullness was clearly in the consciousness of Jesus in the days of his ministry on earth. He testified, "The Father loves the Son and shows him all that he himself is doing" (John 5:20). "All things have been handed over to me by my Father," Jesus declared; "and no one knows the Father except the Son and anyone to whom the Son chooses to reveal him" (Matt. 11:27).

With every new perception of Christ's fullness that we receive, we open ourselves up to be blessed with even more, as Jesus himself testifies: "For to the one who has, more will be given, and he will have an abundance" (Matt. 13:12).

I wonder if there's any theme in Scripture that's both more prevalent on its pages and more overlooked and undervalued by its readers than this fact of the all-encompassing scope of who Christ is.

ALL WE NEED

Throughout Colossians, the divine completeness of Christ is something Paul keeps underscoring in various ways: "For in him the whole fullness of deity dwells bodily" (2:9). In Christ "are hidden all the treasures of wisdom and knowledge" (2:3). In short, "Christ is all" (3:11). *Christ is all*—and all we need.

After seeing and hearing these things about Christ and how praiseworthy he is, to turn and live our lives for anything smaller than Jesus is the height of foolishness. No created thing could ever be for us what the Creator himself alone can be. It makes me think of Francis Schaeffer's words: "If Christ is not Lord *of* all, he's not Lord *at* all."

Why would we ever turn anywhere except to Christ and all his fullness? It isn't remotely reasonable. And yet we do it all the time. Our situation was well captured by C. S. Lewis in these frequently quoted words:

> If we consider the unblushing promises of reward and the staggering nature of the rewards promised in the Gospels, it would seem that our Lord finds our desires not too strong, but too weak. We are half-hearted creatures, fooling about with drink and sex and ambition when infinite joy is offered us, like an ignorant child who wants to go on making mud pies in a slum because he cannot imagine what is meant by an offer of a holiday at the sea. We are far too easily pleased.[8]

We're too easily pleased—and yet in giving ourselves to these meager mud-pie pleasures, we discover only too grievously that we are not in fact "pleased" at all.

That's why our hearts and minds need to be constantly refreshed, not only with the greatness of Christ, but also with the greatness of the gospel.

RECONCILED

As Paul brings this song of Christ's supremacy to a close, he brings the glorious comprehensiveness of Christ to bear at the point where it most fundamentally touches us. It is indeed "through" this Jesus, Paul proclaims, that God will "reconcile to himself *all things*, whether on earth or in heaven, making peace by the blood of his cross" (1:20).

Jesus is mighty to save. Now let's look at the mighty way that he has saved us.

6

NEWS—THE BIGGEST AND BEST

For each of us, the "everything" that Jesus can represent in our lives is always linked, directly and inescapably, to our most basic need—a rescuer to free us from our slavery to sin, from our bondage to self-reliance, and from the burden of our idols. It's a need we never grow out of.

In that summer of 2009, as I fixed my eyes and heart on Paul's letter to the Colossians, one passage meant more than any other. God was showing me the ugly strength of my idolatrous attachment to human approval and the ruinous insecurity and stress this caused. At the same time, he began breaking those chains and setting me free with the astonishing past-tense words of Colossians 1:12: "The Father . . . has *qualified* you to share in the inheritance of the saints in light."

"Tullian," he was telling me, "you're *already qualified!* You don't have to make the grade on your own or seek more approval from anyone. In Christ, you're in!" This God-given qualification also meant a personal share for me in a bright inheritance that could never be diminished or stripped away.

God was opening my eyes to a stunning reappraisal of everything I possessed already in Christ.

I HAD ISSUES

As I came back time and again to Colossians 1, the degree of my slavery was more and more exposed to me, along with the dark depths this had plunged me into—but always with the encouraging strengths of the gospel message to meet me there.

I saw that I had security issues; I recognized how vulnerable and defenseless I felt, so open to attack, and how deeply I ached for more protection. But God was assuring me that my identity, worth, and value had *nothing* to do with my strength or ability to win. It had nothing to do with me at all. It had everything to do with the finished work of Jesus *for* me.

Sweet, emboldening liberation!

He helped me see the certainty of my safety, and the ultimate impregnability of my position, in the next words Paul spoke to the Colossians (past-tense again): "*He has delivered* us from the domain of darkness and *transferred* us to the kingdom of his beloved Son, in whom we have redemption, the forgiveness of sins" (1:13–14).

Tullian, already you've been liberated out of darkness's grip and transported into the kingdom of Jesus; you now are, and forever will be, safe and sound in Jesus—all because of what he long ago accomplished for you.

With that perspective, he reminded me afresh that our struggle is not against flesh and blood but against principalities and powers in the spiritual realm. It helped me identify anew who my real enemy was.

But I had other issues too, I realized. I was worried about my reputation because of all the inaccurate things being said about me. After all, I'd worked hard to gain the good reputation I had, and now it was being questioned and maligned. I was afraid that people I respected (and those I wanted to respect me) were going to think badly of me. I'd come to believe my identity was directly tied to what I could achieve, to who I could become, and to how well people thought of me. It was slavery.

Again, Colossians 1:12 opened my eyes: "The Father . . . has qualified you to share in the inheritance of the saints in light."

Tullian, you're one of the saints in light. You've been united to him; you'll always have his name, his presence, his personality, his reputation overshadowing and filling all that you are in your inmost being. Because Jesus was someone, you're free to be no one.

Here was my identity. It's true I didn't deserve it; it's true it happened only by God's amazing grace to me in Christ; yet it was more deeply and lastingly accurate about me than anything I had accomplished on my own, for myself. It was so freeing to finally realize that, because of Christ's work for me, I didn't have anything to prove or any reputation to protect.

And here's something else with which I was brought face-to-face: with all the turmoil in the church, I came to see how enslaved I felt to a painful situation I desperately wanted to be freed from. I didn't ask for this. And while I had known that blending two churches was going to be hard, I didn't anticipate the level of pain, fear, and isolation I would feel. There was no way I could have foreseen the despair, desperation, and depression I was experiencing. I felt rejected, harassed, and in some sense abandoned. I wanted out. I wanted to be free.

The Colossians passage again spoke volumes to my heart, showing me my true status: "He has delivered us . . . we have redemption."

God reminded me that in Christ I was already free. I was already redeemed—purchased from the slave market of sin and death. The deep liberation I craved, I already had. I was now forever free.

Contrary to what I had thought, I did not need easing circumstances, relief from difficulty, and distance from pain in order to be free. I was learning that the freedom Jesus secured for me is not freedom from pain and suffering here and now. Rather, it's freedom from bitterness, anger, fear, resentment, self-pity, offense, and hopelessness in the crucible of present pain and suffering; it is freedom from my burdensome sense of "I deserve better," the encumbrance of entitlement. I was realizing that only the gospel can free us from the enslaving pressure to defend ourselves. That's *real* freedom—God-sized freedom!

Also, because things had gotten so messy in the church situation, I longed for cleansing, aching to feel unsoiled and restored. The sense of cleansing I needed came through the present-tense words of this same Colossians passage—that in "his beloved Son . . . *we have redemption*, the forgiveness of sins" (vv. 13–14). We have it *now!*

And God said, "Tullian, in my beloved Son, you stand before me this very moment as cleansed, forgiven, purified. Therefore, I will never, ever deal with you on the basis of your cleanliness or dirtiness—your goodness or badness—but on the basis of my Son's finished work on your behalf."

In all this, God wasn't showing me something new; he was helping me rediscover what already is—he was reorienting me to the *now*-power of the gospel. He was reminding me of who I already am in Christ and the benefits that come with being united to him. And I was seeing all this with new eyes; in my dark hour, he was reconnecting my daily life to the light of the gospel.

I love reviewing and reflecting again on those few verses in the first chapter of Colossians that God so strongly used to revive me:

> The Father . . . has qualified you [past tense; it's finished] to share in the inheritance of the saints in light. He has delivered us [past tense again; the deliverance is completed] from the domain of darkness and transferred us [past tense once more:

the transferal is already concluded] to the kingdom of his beloved Son, in whom we have [present tense; this very moment
we possess it] redemption, the forgiveness of sins.

Sometimes God puts us in a position where our only comfort
comes not from what others think about us but from what God
thinks about us in Christ—that we're *forever* qualified, delivered,
loved, accepted, forgiven, clean, and approved. That's where God
had me. I desperately needed a fresh, gospel-soaked reminder of
who I am in Christ—and that's exactly what he gave me.

Because of Christ's finished work, Christians *already* possess
the approval, the love, the security, the freedom, the meaning,
the purpose, the protection, the new beginning, the cleansing,
the forgiveness, the righteousness, and the rescue we intensely
long for and, in fact, look for in a thousand things smaller than
Jesus every day—things transient, things incapable of delivering
the goods.

The gospel is the only thing big enough to satisfy our deepest, eternal longings—both now and forever.

And were it not for that gospel, the *everythingness* of Christ
would remain only a distant, unreachable nothing to us.

GOSPEL GROWTH FOR US ALL

The impact of what I was comprehending in Colossians was
especially intensified by something else I saw in the opening
paragraphs of that epistle.

Early in this letter, Paul mentions "the word of the truth, the
gospel," and he then adds this: "which has come to you, as indeed
in the whole world it is bearing fruit and growing—as it also does
among you" (1:6). He's speaking to Christians, and he tells them
the gospel is not only fruitful and growing around the world, but
in them as well.

It was these verses, specifically, that first convinced me long ago that the gospel is not just for non-Christians. It's bigger than that; it's for Christians, too. The gospel represents both the *nature* of Christian growth and the *basis* for it. Whatever progress we make in our Christian lives—whatever going onward, whatever pressing forward—the direction will always be deeper *into* the gospel, not apart from it, or aside from it. Growth in the Christian life is the process of receiving Christ's "It is finished" into new and deeper parts of our being every day, and it happens as the Holy Spirit daily carries God's good word of justification into our regions of unbelief—what one writer calls our "unevangelized territories."[1]

Paul was telling the Colossians, who in their culture were constantly tempted by contending worldviews and competing offers of salvation and freedom, that only the gospel of Christ has the power to bring about such freedom—such a radical, beautiful rescue. He was saying, "All the liberty and deliverance you long for is yours already in Christ. You don't need to go out and seek it somewhere else, from some other teaching or philosophy or lifestyle. They're selling you counterfeit freedoms, counterfeit deliverances. You already have the *real thing*, so don't buy what you already possess."

Paul was trying to persuade the Colossian Christians not to live beneath the level of the exalted privileges that were theirs *already* in Christ's everythingness.

That was the good news.

MAKING THE NEWS SO GOOD

The reason this news is so vast and wonderful is that the bad news is so huge and horrible. The gospel is big because our sin is big.

You and I will never know Christ to be a great Savior unless we first understand ourselves to be great sinners. We'll never really feel deliverance if we don't first feel desperation. We'll never experience the glory of real freedom if we don't first experience the grief of our own slavery.

In Colossians, Paul comes through clearly with the bad news as well as the good. And to register the right impression with that bad news, he uses some vivid language. Look at what he says: "You . . . once were alienated and hostile in mind, doing evil deeds" (1:21). *Alienated. Hostile. Evil.* Not exactly today's politically correct terminology.

What Paul is describing here is the natural condition of every human being apart from God's saving grace. The Bible makes it clear that we're all born dead in our trespasses and sins, enslaved to ourselves, turned slavishly inward. We learn that each of us comes into this world as an enemy of God (Rom. 5:10). Nobody—not even the cutest child—starts out free, morally neutral, or well-disposed to God. We come into this world needing to be liberated, resurrected, and rescued by God's redeeming grace. What we all justly and rightly deserve—by default, because of our sin—is not God's favor but God's wrath (Eph. 2:1–3). We all begin life alienated from God, relationally estranged from him.

Paul says also in Colossians 1:21 that we were "hostile in mind." It's not a matter of mere indifference; it's outright animosity.

You may respond to Paul's statement with thoughts somewhat like these: "Well, for me, before I was a Christian, I don't ever remember being hostile toward God. It's just that I had no interest; God wasn't anything I thought or cared about." So let me state something clearly: in the Bible, indifference toward God *is* hostility toward him. God gets in the way of what we think we need to be happy and free, so we ignore him—consciously or unconsciously—hoping he'll leave us alone. That's the height of brazen arrogance.

But none of us comes into this world *truly* indifferent toward

God, even though we think we might. Romans 1:18–25 speaks of the universal condition of humanity, telling us that all men and women, boys and girls, have a God-consciousness. All of us have been created in the image of God and therefore inescapably know God at some level. We're vaguely aware of a transcendent need—a thirst—but the effect of sin is such that in and of ourselves we're unable to pinpoint what we're thirsty for or where that thirst can be quenched. Because of sin, we come into this world spending our time and energy suppressing that vague sense of transcendence—that knowledge of God—that's ours. We attempt to drown it out with the fleeting pleasures and pursuits of this world, whatever these may be. We exchange "the glory of the immortal God for images resembling mortal man and birds and animals and creeping things" (Rom. 1:23).

Our ultimate problem, therefore, is not indifference to God but idolatry. Idolatry, according to John Piper, "is a suicidal exchange of infinite value and beauty for some fleeting, inferior substitute." We are, in this sense, suicidal by nature—therefore we need saving from ourselves.

We were all hostile to God, Paul insists, "in mind." Prior to our receiving God's grace in Christ, we were constantly at cross-purposes to him in our thoughts, in our disposition, and in our attitudes. The same was true in our actions. Enmity toward God was manifested in our "doing evil deeds," Paul says.

It's hard for people to accept this description of evil in regard to their own behavior. Were we ever really *that* bad? We think, "I know I've been selfish at times; I may be insensitive and irresponsible now and then. But have my actions ever really been *evil?*" But again, that perspective merely reflects our habitually slackened standards and our failure to fully realize God's rightful demands in light of his perfect glory and holiness and love. Who can say he is not addicted to always wanting to view himself in the best light? And who has ever been in the regular habit of measuring her actions against the holy light of God?

The fact is, the Greek word translated as "evil" in describing our behavior in Colossians 1:21 is the same word used to describe Satan and his demons. It's severe language, for sure. Trust me, we're all a lot worse off than we think we are.

BIG SIN

The bigness of sin comes through in many passages throughout Paul's letters. Romans 5 is one example. Paul describes us as God's "enemies" (v. 10). Sin and its upshot, death, are portrayed as monstrous monarchs: "death *reigned*" (vv. 14, 17), and "sin *reigned* in death" (v. 21). Sin was not only tyrannical in its power but also sweeping in its coverage: "sin came into the world through one man, and death through sin," yet "death *spread to all* men because all sinned" (v. 12). And so it came about that "one trespass led to condemnation for *all* men" (v. 18). Generation after generation, the sin is ceaseless, the death all-encompassing, the condemnation comprehensive.

All this—as Paul knows, and wants us to know—only magnifies the sweet immensity of the "much more" God has done for us through the gospel. Note Paul's many terms of measure and scope and impact in that same Romans 5 passage as he glories in the good news: "*Much more* have the grace of God and the free gift by the grace of that one man Jesus Christ abounded for *many*" (v. 15). "*Much more* will those who receive the *abundance* of grace and the free gift of righteousness reign in life through the one man Jesus Christ" (v. 17). "One act of righteousness leads to justification and life for *all* men" (v. 18). "So that . . . grace also might reign through righteousness leading to *eternal* life through Jesus Christ our Lord" (v. 21).

We find the same startling juxtaposition of the worst possible news with the best in Colossians, to the same effect: "And you, who once were alienated and hostile in mind, doing evil deeds, he has now reconciled in his body of flesh by his death, in order to present you holy and blameless and above reproach before him" (Col. 1:21–22). The distance covered is impossibly, incredibly far—from alienated, hostile, and evil to holy, blameless, and above reproach. This is utterly astonishing. Enormous sin, extravagant gospel.

THE COSMIC REACH

Keep in mind too that just as our sin has had a cosmic extent, so also will the gospel's transforming power extend cosmically.

The breadth of sin is as big as its depth. Paul teaches us in Romans 8 that because humanity's sin has exposed the creative order to futility, "the *whole creation* has been groaning together in the pains of childbirth until now" (v. 22). Because of the "bondage to corruption" (v. 21) forced upon creation by mankind's sin, these groans continually sound forth (and perhaps the great earthquakes that world history has witnessed, including those in our own time, are one of the most direct and tragic manifestations of this). Creation itself is groaning for renewal, begging for Jesus to come back. Creation is singing, *Maranatha! Come, Lord Jesus, come quickly!*

But the gospel's reach, like sin's reach, is cosmic as well. In the same Colossians statement that speaks of how "all the fullness of God" dwells in Christ, Paul adds that "God was pleased . . . through him [Christ] to reconcile to himself all things, whether *on earth or in heaven*, making peace by the blood of his cross" (1:19–20).

He's reconciling everything everywhere.

The scope of Christ's finished work is both individual *and* cosmic: it ranges from personal pardon for sin and individual forgiveness to the final resurrection of our bodies and the restoration of the whole world. Now that's good news—*gospel*—isn't it? If we place our trust in the finished work of Christ, sin's acidic curse will lose its grip on us individually, and we will one day be given a renewed creation. Through Christ's work, our relationship with God is restored while creation itself is renewed. As the beloved Christmas hymn "Joy to the World" puts it:

> He comes to make his blessings flow
> Far as the curse is found.

In these remarkable lines, we broadcast in song a gospel as large as the universe itself. The blessings of redemption flow as far as the curse is found. This hymn reminds us that the gospel is good news to a world that has been twisted, in every imaginable way, beyond the intention of the Creator's design, by the powers of sin and death, but it is a world that God, in Christ, is putting back into shape.

Jesus Christ—and he alone—is the great reconciler, the great mediator. By God's good pleasure and plan, he stood in the gap between the Creator and his estranged creatures, between a sinful people and a holy God. By faith alone, in Christ alone, we who were alienated have now been brought near, relationally reconciled to God the Father, our creator.

We who were hostile have now—solely by faith in Jesus—become "God's chosen ones, holy and beloved" (Col. 3:12). Once we were alienated from our maker; "but now in Christ Jesus you who once were far off have been brought near by the blood of Christ" (Eph. 2:13). Our past behavior can be rightly summarized as "doing evil deeds," but now "we have been sanctified [past tense] through the offering of the body of Jesus Christ once for all" (Heb. 10:10).

In his law-fulfilling life, curse-bearing death, and death-defeating resurrection, Jesus has entirely accomplished for sinners what sinners could never in the least do for themselves. The banner under which the Christian lives reads, "It is finished."

EVERYTHING AND NOTHING

The more we reflect on the gospel, the more we let our hearts and minds soak in it, the more we see how the gospel is saturated with the dynamics of *nothing* and *everything*.

This Jesus who is so infinitely *everything*—this same Jesus "made himself *nothing*" (Phil. 2:7). In Jesus "all the fullness of God was pleased to dwell" (Col. 1:19); nevertheless, "though he was in the form of God," he "did not count equality with God a thing to be grasped" (Phil. 2:6). He "emptied Himself" (v. 7 NASB). The Everything became nothing.

And this is how far it went—here is what God, "for our sake," did through Christ: "He made him to be sin who knew no sin, so that in him we might become the righteousness of God" (2 Cor. 5:21). The Everything became nothing. For our sake.

On the cross, Jesus took upon himself our sin—our corrupt, fatal nothingness—then placed upon us *his righteousness*, his everythingness. It's what has been called "the glorious exchange."

That's the gospel. It takes those who essentially are nothing and have nothing and brings them to a glorious completeness of wholeness and perfection. Not a single one of us could ever have done anything close to that for ourselves—because "we were *dead* in our trespasses" (Eph. 2:5). The next move had to be his. And in love, he made it. "In this the love of God was made manifest among us, that *God sent his only Son into the world*, so that we might live through him" (1 John 4:9).

A restored relationship with God never happens by our climbing up to him; it happens only in Jesus, who came down to us. Grace is descending, one-way love!

Jesus is everything, and, therefore, for mankind the gospel is everything. That's why Paul told the Corinthians that he resolved "to know *nothing* among you *except* Jesus Christ and him crucified" (1 Cor. 2:2). It's why he told the Colossians of his ministry commitment "to make the word of God *fully known*" (Col. 1:25).

This vast gospel, in its fullness, is now ours to fully know, to fully experience, to fully embrace.

PART FOUR

NOTHING

+

7

FULLY EXPOSED

=

Jesus plus nothing equals everything. We've now tackled that equation from back to front. Let's review where this has taken us.

OUR PATH SO FAR

We started with the *everything*. We thought deeply about our desperate, built-in yearning for something more, something huge. The things I crave—and my specific ways of craving them—may not exactly match yours, but we all have them. And for each of us, when we're honest enough to admit it, our must-have list is breathtakingly vast.

Next we explored the tragic *nothingness* we inherit by going after idols. Humanity experiences a deep-rooted restlessness in regard to our cravings, because we're always trying to meet them with something smaller than Jesus. I like how Timothy Keller, in *Counterfeit Gods*, helps us recognize these idols:

> We think that idols are bad things, but that is almost never the case. The greater the good, the more likely we are to expect that it can satisfy our deepest needs and hopes. Anything can serve as a counterfeit god, especially the very best things in life.
>
> What is an idol? It is anything more important to you than God, anything that absorbs your heart and imagination more than God, anything you seek to give you what only God can give.

> A counterfeit god is anything so central and essential to your life that, should you lose it, your life would feel hardly worth living. An idol has such a controlling position in your heart that you can spend most of your passion and energy, your emotional and financial resources, on it without a second thought. . . .
>
> If anything becomes more fundamental than God to your happiness, meaning in life, and identity, then it is an idol.[1]

Keller also insightfully connects this idolatry with the universal cravings we've identified:

> Every human being must live for something. Something must capture our imaginations, our heart's most fundamental allegiance and hope. But, the Bible tells us, without the intervention of the Holy Spirit, that object will never be God himself.[2]

To see this idolatry being played out, Christians don't have to wander into the world; we can see it well enough in our churches, indeed in our own daily lives. Even as believers, we don't adequately realize how Jesus is enough to meet our deepest needs, so we're always pursuing an add-on approach—Jesus *plus* something. All these *somethings* we look to immediately become our idols. They're exactly what God warned us about again and again in Scripture, assuring us of their total worthlessness. But still we pour ourselves into these black holes—especially the deep, dark abyss of what can be called "performancism"—the moralistic legalism that has such a powerful death grip on so many believers and churches and pastors. In *Christless Christianity*, Michael Horton identifies "the regular diet in many churches across America today: 'Do more, try harder.' . . . The focus still seems to be on us and our activity rather than on God and his work in Jesus Christ."[3] This is, indeed, our greatest threat to the gospel.

But then we soaked our hearts and minds in joyful recognition of the mind-blowing immensity of our Savior, *Jesus Christ*, and the comprehensiveness of his saving gospel.

And now, in that still-glowing light of our Savior's sweet and awesome greatness, let's pivot and track back through our equation by proceeding forward to its end. Our next step, then, is to revisit the *nothingness* of our insistent idolatry.

We've seen how our idol addiction is by no means an enjoyable way to live, but in our prideful desire for self-sufficiency we throttle ahead anyway, comforted by the self-stroking illusion that *we have it all together*—or that at least somehow, someday soon, we'll finally get it all together. Meanwhile this approach turns us into ugly beings, our personalities warped by a sense of entitlement that results in chronic complaining (inwardly, at least). We sink into slavery and despair. And the easily noticed repulsiveness of it all ruins the scandalous freedom that Jesus paid so dearly to secure for sinners.

Distasteful stuff, for sure. You're probably not wanting me to drag up any of this again. But the gospel is good reason to keep facing up to our idolatry. The light of God's grace not only exposes idolatry for all its ugliness but also illuminates fully our pathway out of it.

NO LONGER NEEDED

Here's the bottom line. As we allow the Spirit's inner renewing to have its further effect within us, opening ourselves to the fullness of Christ in every way, we realize something extraordinary, something stunning in its freshness and liberation: because of Christ's all-encompassing accomplishment on our behalf through the gospel, *we no longer have even the slightest need for any idol.*

We no longer need to rely (to cite a few alliterated examples) on the position, the prosperity, the promotions, the preeminence, the power, the praise, the passing pleasures, or the popularity that we've so desperately pursued for so long.

Because Jesus has already earned God's full approval and affection and acceptance for us, we no longer require any of that from anyone else. The gospel alone empowers and emboldens us to press on and strain forward with no anxiety over gaining other people's sanction or good opinion—even God's! All the care and love and value we most crave—full and final approval—we already have in Jesus.

The same is true for the meaning and purpose and validation and direction and freedom and security that all of us long for. His sacrifice for us has earned all this for us directly from God. With those idols no longer burdening our lives, we're suddenly freed and empowered to live a life of outrageous generosity, unrestrained sacrifice, uncommon boldness, and unbounded nerve.

This miracle is made possible because of our being united with Christ, the great "in him" doctrine that's taught so profoundly in such passages as John 15, and Ephesians 1, and Romans 6 and 8.

In the New Testament's original Greek, Ephesians 1:3–14 is one long sentence. Paul there becomes so overwhelmed by the sheer greatness and immensity and size and sweetness of God's amazing grace that he doesn't even take a breath. He writes in a state of controlled ecstasy. And at the heart of his elation is this idea of union with Christ. We have been blessed, he writes, "in Christ with every spiritual blessing" (v. 3). He says we've been chosen, graced, redeemed, reconciled, destined, and sealed forever in Christ (vv. 4–13). The everything we need and long for, Paul says, we already possess if we are in Christ. Our Savior has already sweepingly secured all that we crave and deeply need.

We see the same thing—this great "in him" doctrine—beautifully set forth in Colossians as well. Here Paul shows how union with Christ is the foundation of all our spiritual experience. Paul's committed goal in his work of ministry is to "present everyone mature *in Christ*" (1:28). He reminds us that just as we received Christ as Lord, so we're also privileged to "walk *in him*, rooted and built up *in him*" (2:6–7). Paul assures us that we've been "filled *in him*" (2:10). He speaks with gospel richness of how "*in him* also" we received a spiritual and supernatural "circumcision" that embraces our "having been buried *with him* in baptism, in which you were also raised *with him* through faith in the powerful working of God, who raised him from the dead"; consequently God has made us "alive together *with him*, having forgiven us all our trespasses" (2:12–13). In the same vein, he later reminds his readers that their very lives are "*hidden with Christ* in God" (3:3).

Expanding this concept of our union with Christ, we also see wonderfully expressed in Colossians the other aspect of the "in him" doctrine, which is *he in us*. Paul equates "Christ in you" with our "hope of glory"; he assures that it's a "mystery" that God is making known among the nations; he tells us it's a mystery of "glory"; he says the glory contains "riches"; and he insists that the riches are indeed "great" (1:27). What he speaks of here, what he wants us to grasp, is wonderful and weighty and intensely high and marvelous. In *The Gospel-Driven Life,* Michael Horton helps open our eyes to all that "in Christ" means:

> Paul does not say, "Be like Jesus." He says, "You *are* like Jesus." . . . It's easy for us to rely on the gospel for forgiveness and justification but then to look elsewhere for our renewal and sanctification. However, Paul says that it's all there: "in Christ." Only after saying this does Paul then issue the imperative to live a life that is consistent with this truth. . . . Being in Christ is the perpetual source of our becoming like Christ, not vice versa.[4]

DAILY REMINDERS

All this becomes more accessible and embraceable for us as we do something Jerry Bridges advises: preaching the gospel to yourself every day.[5] Because we're so naturally prone to look to ourselves and our performance more than we look to Christ and his performance, we need constant reminders of the gospel.

If we're supposed to preach the gospel to ourselves every day, what's the actual content of that message? What is it exactly that we need to keep reminding ourselves of?

If God has saved you—if he's given you the faith to believe, and you're now a Christian, if you've transferred trust from your own accomplishments and abilities to Christ's accomplishment on behalf of sinners—then here's the good news. In the phraseology of Colossians 1, it's simply this: you've already been qualified, you've already been delivered, you've already been transferred, you've already been redeemed, and you've already been forgiven.

Day by day, what God wants us to experience *practically* only happens as we come to a deeper understanding of what we are *positionally*—a deeper understanding of what's already ours in Christ.

I used to think that growing as a Christian meant I had to somehow go out and obtain the qualities and attitudes I was lacking. To really mature, I needed to find a way to get more joy, more patience, more faithfulness, and so on.

Then I came to the shattering realization that this isn't what the Bible teaches, and it isn't the gospel. What the Bible teaches is that we mature as we come to a greater realization of what we *already* have in Christ. The gospel, in fact, transforms us precisely because it's not itself a message about our internal transformation but about Christ's external substitution. We desperately need an advocate, mediator, and friend. But what we need most is a substitute—someone who has done for us and secured for us what we could never do and secure for ourselves.

The hard work of Christian growth, therefore, is to think less of ourselves and our performance and more of Jesus and his performance for us. Ironically, when we focus mostly on our need to get better, we actually get worse. We become neurotic and self-absorbed. Preoccupation with our effort instead of with God's effort for us makes us increasingly self-centered and morbidly introspective.

Again, think of it this way: sanctification is the daily hard work of going back to the reality of our justification. It's going back to the certainty of our objectively secured pardon in Christ and hitting the refresh button a thousand times a day. Or, as Martin Luther so aptly put it in his *Lectures on Romans*, "To progress is always to begin again." Real spiritual progress, in other words, requires a daily going backwards.

In *Because He Loves Me*, Elyse Fitzpatrick writes about how important remembrance is in Christian growth:

> One reason we do not grow in ordinary, grateful obedience as we should is that we've got amnesia; we've forgotten that we were cleansed from our sins. In other words, he is saying that on-going failure in our sanctification (the slow process of change into Christlikeness) is the direct result of failing to remember God's love for us in the gospel. If we lack the comfort and assurance that his love and cleansing are meant to supply, our failures will handcuff us to yesterday's sins, and we won't have faith or courage to fight against them, or the love for God that's meant to empower this war. Please don't miss the import of Peter's statement. *If we fail to remember our justification, redemption, and reconciliation, we will struggle in our sanctification.*[6]

Christian growth, in other words, doesn't happen by first behaving better, but by believing better—believing in bigger, deeper, brighter ways what Christ has already secured for sinners.

Realizing this has changed the entire way I read the Bible.

Think of what Paul tells us in Philippians 2:12: "Work out your own salvation with fear and trembling." We've got work to do—but what exactly is it? Get better? Try harder? Pray more? Get more involved in church? Read the Bible longer? What *precisely* is Paul exhorting us to do? He goes on to explain: "For it is God who works in you, both to will and to work for his good pleasure" (v. 13). God works *his* work in *you*, which is the work already accomplished by Christ. Our hard work, therefore, means coming to a greater understanding of *his* work.

And so it is that we move further into the gospel, into a deeper, bigger, brighter understanding of all that God has already achieved for us in Christ. By continuing to place your trust in Christ's finished work, and by learning to do this more and more, all that he's secured for sinners—all that is your possession already in fact—now becomes increasingly yours in experience. You keep savoring the riches of God's pardon and power as your heritage forever in Christ.

As we better grasp the gospel of grace, we come to see that Jesus came not as an angry tyrant to strip away our freedom but as an affectionate friend and deliverer to strip away our slavery to lesser things, so that we might become truly free. We learn from the gospel that being a slave to Christ is the essence of freedom, while being abandoned to self (which is what our culture is constantly pushing) is the essence of slavery.

By daily preaching this gospel to ourselves, we can more readily see and confront all the idols in our lives—including those we may not be quite as aware of. We will be able to recognize that every temptation to sin is a temptation to not believe the gospel—the temptation to secure for ourselves something we think we need in order to be happy, something we don't yet have: meaning, liberty, validation, and so on. When we succumb to temptation, we are failing to believe in that moment that everything we need, in Christ we already have. Real freedom happens when the rich resources of the gospel smash any sense of need to secure for ourselves anything beyond what Christ has already secured for us.

THE BRIGHTEST FREEDOM

One aspect in which the gospel's glorious freedom can continue to shine brightest for us is in how it gives the death blow to legalism. We've already discussed at some length this dreadful thing we can call "legalism" or "performancism" or "moralism." But because it's such a cruel, subtle, and pervasive danger in our lives and in the church, it's worth focusing on a little more. As Michael Horton observes, "A church that is deeply aware of its misery and nakedness before a holy God will cling tenaciously to an all-sufficient Savior, while one that is self-confident and relatively unaware of its inherent sinfulness will reach for religion and morality whenever it seems convenient."[7]

The gospel is the only thing that can crush our legalistic tendencies and break their chains, since the gospel keeps returning our focus not on what we must achieve but on what Christ has already finished.

When it comes to drawing near to God and pleasing him, legalism insists that *obedience precedes acceptance*—that it's all up to us. But the fresh breeze of gospel freedom announces that *acceptance precedes obedience*—that once we're already approved and already accepted by God in Christ, we can freely follow God's lead and grow in doing his will out of genuine gratitude for his amazing grace and without any fear of judgment or condemnation when we fail.

C. S. Lewis observed that what most distinguishes the gospel from legalism is that legalism says God will love us if we are good, while the gospel tells us God *will make us good* because he loves us. That's a big difference—and getting your heart and mind around it will change your life. In the light of gospel grace, we're liberated by the recognition that God loves us in order to make us lovely, not because we *are* lovely (we know we really aren't) or could ever be lovely on our own. Love precedes loveliness in God's economy; and his love is plenty big enough to actuate within us all the loveliness we could ever dream of.

Legalism keeps insisting that Christianity is all about how we perform for God; the gospel keeps proclaiming that Christianity, ever and always, is all about how God in Christ performs for us. When we transfer trust from self-performance to Christ and his performance, we finally leap out from under the burden of having to measure up on our own.

AVOIDING JESUS

In light of the gospel, let me especially demolish the myth that legalism is a blunder that's associated only with our initial salvation—with our positional justification in God's eyes. Most believers realize we could never earn such salvation; we've come to accept that no one can work his way into God's kingdom. We know that. Most of us who read the Bible believe that to be true.

But when it comes to our sanctification, suddenly we become legalists. In the matter of maturing in Christlikeness—and in continuing to please God and find favor with God and acceptance with God—we suppose it's all about what we have to accomplish ourselves and all the rules and standards and values we need to adhere to. We seem to inherently assume that our performance is what will finally determine whether our relationship with God is good or bad: so much good behavior from us generates so much affection from God; or so much bad behavior from us generates so much anger from God.

We get the Christian life all backwards. It subtly becomes all about us and what we do (which leads to slavery) instead of being all about Jesus and what's he's done (which leads to freedom). We may not articulate all this theologically, but it sure comes out in the way we live.

By their behavior, legalists essentially are saying this: "I live the Christian life by the rules—rules that I establish for myself as well as those I expect others to abide by." They develop specific requirements of behavior beyond what the Bible teaches, and they make observance of those requirements the means by which they judge the acceptability of others in the church.

We've all become pretty adept at establishing these rules and standards that we find personally achievable. Legalism therefore provides us with a way to avoid acknowledging our deficiencies and our inabilities. That's enough right there to make it attractive to us. But it's also appealing to us in how it puffs us up, giving us the illusion (as we've seen) that *we can do it*—we can generate our own meaning, our own purpose, our own security, and all our other inmost needs. It's what Michael Horton pinpoints as "the default setting of the human heart: the religion of self-salvation."[8]

It's all so attractive because it's *all about us*. Legalism feeds our natural pride. While abiding by our self-established standards and rules, we think pretty highly of ourselves. It's a gratifying arrangement because it allows us (we think) to control our little world, to protect ourselves from the chaos without. And what's especially fine about being in charge of our situation (though we wouldn't admit it) is that it's a way to avoid Jesus.

Because our self-imposed rules make us feel safe and self-pleased, they become a counterfeit God, a substitute savior. We morph Christianity into something that focuses exclusively on externals and behavior—which is *not* Christianity and *not* the gospel. Legalism is detached from what Paul likes to call "the gospel of the *grace* of God" (Acts 20:24). "Grace is primarily seen by evangelicals," writes Michael Horton, "as divine *assistance* for the process of moral transformation rather than as a one-sided divine *rescue*."[9]

Tragically, we fail to see that we're turning our backs on grace. Grace is antithetical to legalism; and because God loves to extend his grace, he's a hater of legalism.

ALWAYS OFFENSIVE

If you're uncomfortable with what I'm saying here, don't take it up with me; take it up with the writers of the New Testament. The message of grace they proclaim is as plain as day.

The fact is, their message offends us all. It offends our natural tendencies to be self-centered, to be preferential, to be proud, to be greedy. The gospel is intended to wrestle us to the ground and to crush our idols, and we all, by nature, resist that in certain ways. You're a legalist, I'm a legalist, and we all need the gospel to crush it in our lives.

This is mankind's age-old problem. "The gospel is an offense at precisely the same points and for the same reasons as always," Michael Horton says. "The gospel is so counterintuitive to our fallen pride that it cannot be believed apart from a miracle of divine grace."[10] And again, this is true not just before we become Christians but also afterward.

In our offense at the gospel of grace, we put up a smoke screen. We're afraid that if we went *that* overboard into all this "abounding grace," it would only unleash more sinful actions on our part. That's an issue Paul tackled, of course: "What shall we say then? Are we to continue in sin that grace may abound?" (Rom. 6:1). It's a question he knew would arise as he proclaimed the gospel of grace in his words to the Roman believers. Should we sin all the more to experience grace all the more? Paul answered this at once—and with further gospel truth: "By no means! *How can we who died to sin still live in it?*" (v. 2). The only reason Christians raise the why-not-keep-on-sinning question is that they don't fully understand the gospel. What licentious people need is a greater understanding of grace, not a governor on grace.

Contrary to what we would naturally conclude, the antidote to lawlessness isn't more rules but a deeper grasp of God's grace. The irony of real growth in godliness is that those who end up obeying more are those who increasingly realize that their standing with God isn't based on their obedience for Jesus but on Jesus's obedience for them. Michael Horton comments this way on Paul's message here in this part of Romans:

> If the full remission of sins and favor with God is the believer's possession through faith alone, and God's grace is greater than our sin, why shouldn't we go on sinning? That is the question that Paul knew his teaching on justification would provoke. His answer, in Romans 6, is that the same Good News that announces our justification also announces our death, burial, and resurrection with Christ. Paul does not threaten with the fears of purgatorial fires or worse, but simply declares to those who believe in Christ that he is not only the source of their justification but of their deliverance from sin's all-controlling dominion.[11]

FOOLISH OR FREE?

God hates legalism. That message sounds throughout the Bible, and it's certainly a major theme of Paul's, especially in his letter to the Galatians. Legalism insists that my ongoing relationship with God is based on my ability to do good. That approach is always inconsistent with the gospel, and Paul shoots it down in every letter he writes—both through the way he structures those letters and in their content.

Paul labels this approach as foolishness. His message is basically this: God hates legalism because it's our attempt to stand on our own righteousness in outright disrespect and disregard and misunderstanding of God's righteousness. Moreover, it violates his loving intention to make us free. In our pride, we'd far rather rely on our own righteousness than on the "alien" righteousness, the outside righteousness, that God freely and willingly applies to us through the gospel—the righteousness of Jesus.

In his letter to the Galatians, especially in chapter 1, Paul uses the strongest terms possible in exhorting believers to go back to the gospel as the one and only basis for their Christian lives. Later he launches a series of rhetorical questions to jolt their thinking on this. He takes them back to the beginning of their Christian experience, the essence of which never changes. "Let me ask you only this," he says. "Did you receive the Spirit by works of the law or by hearing with faith?" (Gal. 3:2). It was, of course, always the second, never the first. Paul equates the "works of the law" with by-the-flesh futility, and he says the same dynamic is true in our going forward in the Christian life. "Are you so foolish?" Paul asks. "Having begun by the Spirit, are you now being perfected by the flesh?" (v. 3). In other words, having trusted in Christ's work to *get* you in, are you now trusting in your work to *keep* you in? Paul is helping them return to the truth: the Christian life begins with the Spirit's work, it continues in the Spirit's work, and it culminates by the Spirit's work.

Paul drills ahead with more questioning: "Does he who supplies the Spirit to you and works miracles among you do so by works of the law, or by hearing with faith?" (v. 5). Spirit enablement and miracle working—this is exactly what's required for our sanctification, just as it is for our conversion and our glorification. First to last, faith *alone* (which is itself a gift from God) in Christ's finished work alone—not our work—is the essence of our right response to God's grace. By faith alone we believe and are saved; by faith alone we're sanctified; by faith alone we shall be glorified. As Paul will state a bit later, it is "through the Spirit, by faith" that "we ourselves eagerly wait for the hope of righteousness" (Gal. 5:5).

Paul goes on to declare, "For freedom Christ has set us free," and that must include letting go of the burden of having to "become a better you." Paul therefore commands, with apostolic authority, "Stand firm therefore, and do not submit again to a yoke of slavery" (5:1). And in what may be the hardest hitting lines of the letter, he pronounces the upshot of their tragic love affair with legalism: "You are severed from Christ . . . ; you have fallen away from grace" (v. 4). Isn't it interesting that in this verse Paul describes falling from grace not in terms of immorality or godless living but as legalism—a "do more, try harder" performancism? He urgently wants them to see that we're justified by grace alone, we're sanctified by grace alone, and we're glorified by grace alone. There's no other way. The Christian life is all of a piece, all fully woven in the Spirit by grace through faith.

As Michael Horton writes in *The Gospel-Driven Life*, "What we need most, not just at the beginning, but in the middle and at the end of the Christian journey, is *good news*."[12]

Expanding on a famous line from William Temple in the nineteenth century, I like to remind myself and others that *the only thing you contribute to your salvation and to your sanctification is the sin that makes them necessary.* I hope that helps us understand the radical necessity of daily grace. Our daily sin requires a daily distribution of it.

Grace's good news—always welcome, always refreshing for us—is that *for freedom Christ has set us free*, and he intends to keep us free. His amazing grace has loosened our chains; our shackles no longer hold us back. We must lay aside the sin that so easily entangles us, the sin of "submitting again to a yoke of slavery," the enslaving stress of having to make something out of ourselves. When we transfer trust from our success to Christ's success for us, we experience the abundant freedoms that come from not having to measure up.

And this indeed we *can* do, but only in the light of the gospel.

8

OUT OF THE SHADOWS

As a stronghold of subtle idolatry, legalism in any form must be anti-gospel because it enslaves in its presumption that life is all about us and our abilities. But the gospel, we know, insists that true life is all about Jesus and what he's already done. In its widest sweep, the gospel accentuates what Jesus has done, is doing, and will do; it assuredly does not lay emphasis on anything we must do.

Paul's teaching in Colossians helped open my eyes wider to more facets of this truth and to legalism's sinister threat.

RESCUE FROM NOTHINGNESS

We've discussed how the Colossian believers were being sucked into a slough of nothingness; false teachers had arisen amid them, pointing them away from Jesus. They were tempting them away from him with the promise of something better—a deeper salvation, a better rescue, enhanced freedom, more enlightened knowledge, and heightened power that went beyond anything Christ had done or could do for them. These ideas apparently sprang from several sources: Greek philosophy, Jewish traditions, and even pagan folk beliefs. What they all had in common was a shrunken view of Christ's sufficiency and supremacy.

To fight this evil influence, Paul's strategy unfolds impressively in the first two chapters of Colossians. Let's follow that strategy and especially consider how it might apply to our own strategy against idolatry and legalism.

Paul makes a genuine personal connection with his readers as he begins, reminding them of his ministry on their behalf, as well as targeting their fatal attraction to the "nothingness" that they were being enticed by. We've seen that he sets forth Christ in a vibrant, vivid light, and the more closely we observe and reflect on his words, the more we recognize just how much the supremacy and sufficiency of Christ are controlling the core of Paul's heart and mind. We also recognize how deeply it must grieve him to know of believers who seek to satisfy their inner needs in some way other than through Christ.

Throughout this letter, Paul keeps mentioning the concept of fullness and *allness* in various ways. As you and I observe these usages more closely, think about the particular ways Paul is stretching their understanding of Christ into wider dimensions.

Just after the letter's opening, Paul assures them, "We have not ceased to pray for you, asking that you may be *filled* with the knowledge of his will in all spiritual wisdom and understanding, so as to walk in a manner worthy of the Lord, *fully* pleasing to him, bearing fruit in *every* good work and *increasing* in the knowledge of God. May you be strengthened with *all* power, according to his glorious might, for *all* endurance and patience with joy" (Col. 1:9–11). Whatever yearnings the Colossians experience for a richer, fuller spiritual life, there can be no doubt this is Paul's desire for them as well.

Paul then quickly turns their attention to the one who alone is fully qualified to meet their desire for more fullness. He exalts the *everythingness* of Christ in the melodic passage we observed earlier:

> He is . . . the firstborn of *all* creation. For by him *all* things were created . . . *all* things were created through him and for him. And

he is before *all* things, and in him *all* things hold together. . . . He is the beginning . . . that in *everything* he might be preeminent. For in him *all* the *fullness* of God was pleased to dwell, and through him to reconcile to himself *all* things. (Col. 1:15–20)

Concentrating on the gospel, Paul even notes how it "has been proclaimed in *all* creation under heaven" (Col. 1:23), as he further highlights the comprehensiveness of the good news of Christ.

UNCONFINED

While writing this letter, Paul sits in a Roman prison, the direct consequence of his bold apostolic ministry for Christ and the gospel of grace. But even this confinement can't curb his fullness theme as he tells the Colossians, "I rejoice in my sufferings for your sake, and in my flesh I am *filling* up what is lacking in Christ's afflictions for the sake of his body, that is, the church" (v. 24). He also declares afresh his ministry goal: "to make the word of God *fully* known" (v. 25). He's wholly engaged in an expansive vocation from God, who "chose to make known how great among the Gentiles are the riches of the glory of this mystery, which is Christ in you, the hope of glory" (v. 27).

Paul's awareness of comprehensiveness embraces his total ministry approach and calling. He proclaims Christ, "warning everyone and teaching everyone with all wisdom, that we may present everyone mature ["complete," "perfect"] in Christ. For this I toil, struggling with *all* his energy that he powerfully works within me" (vv. 28–29).

Then Paul gets more focused on the specific situation in Colossae. Paul had apparently learned the details of the problems in the Colossian church from a man named Epaphras, who about a decade earlier seems to have been the initial founder of the Colossian church (see Col. 1:7; 4:12–13), and who was now in prison with Paul (see Philem. 23).

So Paul is fully aware of their condition—and deeply troubled by it. In the opening verse of Colossians 2 he writes, "I want you to know how great a struggle I have for you and for those at Laodicea." Laodicea was a nearby city where apparently Epaphras had also founded a church. Paul completes this sentence in an eye-catching way: ". . . how great a struggle I have for you . . . and for *all* who have not seen me face to face." Paul viewed his prayer focus as extending to the entire body of believers everywhere, including the many throughout the world who had never seen or heard or known him. What an example for us to give a wider scope to our own prayers!

Something bigger may be implied in this last phrase as well. Paul seems to recognize how the turning-aside-from-Christ temptation to which the Colossian believers were falling prey was a demonic strategy against the entire church everywhere. And so it continues even today.

After demonstrating his deep and prayerful concern about this, Paul hammers home his specific message, stressing their urgent need to turn to Christ for true fulfillment. He says his expanded prayer for the believers is this: "That their hearts may be encouraged, being knit together in love, to reach all the riches of full assurance of understanding and the knowledge of God's mystery, which is Christ, in whom are hidden *all* the treasures of wisdom and knowledge" (2:2–3). Jesus has everything they could ever possibly need; their calling is to lay hold of those grace riches, totally, absolutely, exclusively.

EXPOSING A DELUSION

Paul then confronts the false teachers more directly. He declares to the Colossians that he's saying these things about Christ "in order that no one may delude you with plausible arguments" (Col. 2:4). The false teachers' offers of fulfillment outside of

Christ may seem reasonable and believable, but they're nevertheless nothing more than delusions.

Despite the depth of his concerns and the severity of his warning, Paul is a model of graciousness in his approach (fully reflecting the loving appeal of the gospel of grace). He locates evidence of God's grace at work in their lives and genuinely commends them for it: "For though I am absent in body, yet I am with you in spirit, rejoicing to see your good order and the firmness of your faith in Christ" (v. 5).

He recalls the gospel grace they've already tasted and gently reminds them that this alone is where they need to look again to shape and direct their lives: "As you received Christ Jesus the Lord, so walk in him, rooted and built up in him and established in the faith, just as you were taught, abounding in thanksgiving" (vv. 6–7).

Then again he touches on the false teachers and their danger: "See to it that no one takes you captive by philosophy and empty deceit, according to human tradition, according to the elemental spirits of the world, and not according to Christ" (v. 8). He's exposing the reality of what the Colossians were being offered in the teaching they found so attractive.

Paul says this teaching is *enslaving*—don't be taken captive by it, he warns. He adds that it's also *empty* ("hollow" NIV). Ultimately, there was nothing to it.

It's also *deceitful*—all counterfeit.

And it's merely *human*, without any higher source, despite its spiritually pretentious appearances. Then as now, there's never a shortage of enthralling human traditions and philosophies to arrest our minds and hearts and turn them away from solid truth.

Paul adds that this false teaching is merely earthly, worldly— "according to the elemental spirits of the world." That phrase is unusual and its meaning variously interpreted; it's also translated as "the basic principles of this world" (NIV); "the ruling spirits of this world" (NCV); "the spiritual powers of this world" (NLT); and "elemental forces of the world" (HCSB), to mention a few variations. The wording apparently points to the overarching ethos of the world, how this world operates, the world system; it also calls to mind dark, vacuous depths, the essence of deadly, undesirable nothingness. We remember again how Satan is "the ruler of this world" (John 12:31; 14:30; 16:11); and that "the whole world lies in the power of the evil one" (1 John 5:19).

THE WORST FAULT

As Paul lists these defects of the teaching the Colossians were drawn to, he reserves his most important and impassioned point in 2:8 for last: this false teaching is directly opposed to the Savior—it is "not according to Christ." Christ alone is the standard by which all teachings and traditions and philosophies and worldviews and lifestyle approaches must be judged, and the enticements that the Colossians were so taken with did not even begin to measure up.

All this is what the false teachers were selling. *Don't buy it*, Paul insists. These powerful worldly allurements were as attractive to them as they are to us today. But ultimately they're void of any value. However formidable and substantial these things may seem now, their utter nothingness will be brought out eventually, because God himself has determined to do it—he has chosen "*to bring to nothing* things that are, so that no human being might boast in the presence of God" (1 Cor. 1:28–29).

In stark contrast to Paul's portrayal of the empty, deceitful charms of the false teachers, in the next verses he again declares how in Christ "the whole *fullness* of deity dwells bodily," and he pinpoints what this full gospel of this full Christ means for believers: "You have been *filled* in him, who is the head of *all* rule and authority" (Col. 2:9–10).

And then—for the Colossians' sake as well as for ours—Paul gives to the gospel one of its most wonderful and profound expressions in all of Scripture, helping us better see the incredible miracle that has happened:

> In him [in Christ] . . . you were circumcised with a circumcision made without hands, by putting off the body of the flesh, by the circumcision of Christ, having been buried with him in baptism, in which you were also raised with him through faith in the powerful working of God, who raised him from the dead. And you, who were dead in your trespasses and the uncircumcision of your flesh, God made alive together with him, having forgiven us all our trespasses, by canceling the record of debt that stood against us with its legal demands. This he set aside, nailing it to the cross. He disarmed the rulers and authorities and put them to open shame, by triumphing over them in him. (vv. 11–15)

From deadness to aliveness, and from saturation in trespasses to immersion in forgiveness—that's our journey in the gospel. The images here are starkly vivid and unforgettable: flesh and circumcision; burial; a written indictment nailed to a cross; powerful forces disarmed and publically shamed.

In my Bible, I've written the words *the gospel!* in the margin alongside verses 13 and 14 of Colossians 2, and I've put brackets around those two verses. In rich terms, they represent a concise summary of the essence of the gospel. Allow me to repeat these liberating words:

> And you, who were dead in your trespasses and the uncircumcision of your flesh, God made alive together with him, having forgiven us all our trespasses, by canceling the record of debt that stood against us with its legal demands. This he set aside, nailing it to the cross.

Paul uses these words very intentionally here.

ON THE VICTOR'S SIDE

In this passage's climax, the final note is one of triumph. Christ alone is the victor, and sharing in his victory is our only hope of ever being on the truly winning side. Moreover, those whom Christ has defeated are precisely the sources of the false teaching that the Colossians were drawn to, as we can easily gather from what Paul has told us earlier.

It's as if he's asking the Colossians, Whose side do you really want to be on—Christ's or Satan's? Will you stand with the Victor, or grovel beside his disgraced, enfeebled foes? That's the choice we all face.

ONLY SHADOWS

Paul isn't through pressing his case. There's so much to say about all this! There is so much that's wrong in the message of the false teachers and so infinitely much that's good and right and perfect in the gospel of grace and in the Lord and Savior it presents.

Paul next issues the Colossian believers an apostolic command, as he drills to the heart of the legalism issue and deals it a death blow. "Therefore let *no one* pass judgment on you in questions of food and drink, or with regard to a festival or a new moon or a Sabbath" (2:16). The items here have to do with Old Testament religious rituals, and Paul could have listed plenty more (he, as a former Pharisee, would be able to go on and on about this). But he quickly gets to the point. Why should the Colossians refuse to let a teacher or anyone else enforce upon them these regulations? Because "these are a shadow of the things to come, but the substance belongs to Christ" (v. 17).

In the Old Testament, the various dietary and ceremonial regulations, plus the instructions for various feasts and commemorations, plus all the other various rules for sacrifices and worship and relationships and community and national life—all these things were pointing to something higher, something beyond themselves. And that something was the Messiah, Jesus Christ.

All those detailed directives in the Old Testament were merely "a shadow" of the realities to be found in Christ. And while the "shadows" were good in that they show us something of who God truly is, they were still shadowy in their revelation of God. As Hebrews 1:1–3 says: "Long ago, at many times and in many ways, God spoke to our fathers by the prophets, but in these last days he has spoken to us by his Son, whom he appointed the heir of all things, through whom also he created the world. He is the radiance of the glory of God and the *exact* imprint of his nature." In other words, there's a body that casts the shadows—and that body, that "substance," is Jesus himself.

Paul's reasoning here coincides with what we see in the epistle to the Hebrews. The writer there reminds us that the Old Testament priests "serve *a copy and shadow* of the heavenly things" (8:5). Later in Hebrews we read that the law itself "*has but a shadow* of the good things to come instead of the true form of these realities" (10:1). In the Old Testament, God had revealed himself through types and shadows, through promises and prophecies. In the New Testament, God reveals himself in Jesus— who's the substance of every shadow and the fulfillment of every promise and prophecy.

Paul's point in Colossians 2:17 is this: every Old Testament law—the ceremonial laws, civil laws, and dietary laws—were pointers to Jesus. All those things were intended to foreshadow Jesus, to ready us for Christ, to point us forward to our need for Jesus. The law was never intended to be an end in itself but a means to an end. Therefore, focusing on rules and regulations means *missing Jesus altogether*. It's exactly what the Pharisees did.

Think about this as not only concerning your relationship with God but also regarding your relationships with your spouse and children, with friends and neighbors and coworkers, and with others in your church. Whenever we find ourselves focusing primarily (almost exclusively sometimes—at least, I'm guilty of that) on an expectation of rules and standards and values, and we're imposing those things on others, then we're building our life on shadows; we're missing the substance. We're missing the point, which is always Jesus.

The Bible's portrayal of these things as *shadowy* also implies their brief transience in great contrast to Christ. God the Father says to Jesus his Son, "Your throne, O God, is forever and ever" (Heb. 1:8). Reigning eternally, Jesus alone possesses the eternal resources we need to satisfy our eternal yearnings. That's why looking to anything or anyone smaller than Jesus to save us is an exercise in futility.

USELESS

Paul goes on, this time bringing up a different kind of list: "Let no one disqualify you, insisting on asceticism and worship of angels, going on in detail about visions, puffed up without reason by his sensuous mind" (Col. 2:18). Here the focus is not on Jewish religious observances but on a wide variety of spiritual practices with a wider origin, including pagan sources. But the false teachers were "insisting on" these things, just as they did various Jewish religious regulations; without doing these things, they said, you simply weren't qualified spiritually.

Paul's response is still to bring in the contrast of Christ and to contend that true human fulfillment comes only from him. Paul says that teachers who push those worldly spiritual practices are "not holding fast to the Head, from whom the whole body, nourished and knit together through its joints and ligaments, grows with a growth that is from God" (v. 19). Christ alone is the source of everyone's true spiritual maturity, the only source of the growth that originates from God.

Once more Paul takes them back to their gospel foundation: "With Christ you died to the elemental spirits of the world" (v. 20). There's that word "elemental" again—likely referring once more to the dark forces and principles of worldliness. If you died to such things, Paul asks the Colossians, "why, as if you were still alive in the world, do you submit to regulations—'Do not handle, Do not taste, Do not touch' (referring to things that all perish as they are used)—according to human precepts and teachings?" (vv. 20–22). Why submit to enslavement by worldly rules of any kind when Christ's death (which you share in) has set you free from that kind of control?

SECOND THINGS FIRST

We Christians have a remarkable tendency to focus almost exclusively on the fruit of the problem. We do this as parents with our children, pastors with our parishioners, husbands with wives and wives with husbands. We do this with ourselves. The gospel, on the other hand, always addresses the root of the problem. And the root of the problem is not bad behavior. Bad behavior is the fruit of something deeper.

Like Paul, Harold Senkbeil rightly identifies our real enemy: death. Sins, in other words, are the fruit of a much deeper problem, a problem that only God can solve. Death is the root of the problem.

> "This looks good," she thought to herself. Such shiny fruit; it fairly cried out to be eaten, to be enjoyed. And what a broadening experience such enjoyment would be—the knowledge of good and evil, the Mighty One had said. How could He want less than the very best for His own?
>
> "My husband and I will be like God Himself," she reflected. "Now, could that be so bad?"
>
> The serpent made sense: it would be much better to know both good and evil than to know only good.

"Here, have some." She handed the juicy pulp to her husband.

"This is good stuff. By the way, Adam, do you know what God meant by that word—I think it was 'die?'"[1]

All sinful behavior—even in Christians—can be traced back to the death that happened in Eden. To address behavior without addressing death is to perpetuate death. The Pharisees were masters of this, and Jesus called them "white-washed tombs." Many of us Christians are guilty of making this same mistake. We tend to think of the gospel as God's program to make bad people good, not dead people alive. The fact is, Jesus came first to effect a mortal resurrection, not a moral reformation, as his own death and resurrection demonstrate.

The following excerpt is from Senkbeil's excellent article in *Justified: Modern Reformation Essays on the Doctrine of Justification*:

> Most people think that the human dilemma is that our lives are out of adjustment; we don't meet God's expectations. Salvation then becomes a matter of rearranging our priorities and adjusting our life-style to correspond with God's will. In its crassest form, this error leads people to think they earn their own salvation. More often in today's evangelical world, the error has a more subtle disguise: armed with forgiveness through Jesus, people are urged to practice the techniques and principles Christ gave to bring their life-style back into line.
>
> It is certainly true that sinful lives are out of adjustment. We are all in need of the Spirit's sanctifying power. But that comes only after our real problem is solved. Sins are just the symptom; our real dilemma is death.
>
> God warned Adam and Eve that the knowledge of evil came with a high price tag: ". . . when you eat of (the tree of the knowledge of good and evil) you will surely die" (Gen. 2:17). Our first parents wanted to be like God and were willing to pay the price. And we are still paying the price: "the wages of sin

is death . . . " (Rom. 6:23); ". . . in Adam all die" (1 Cor. 15:22); ". . . You were dead in your transgressions and sins" (Eph. 2:1).

The real problem we all face is death. Physical death, to be sure. But ultimately and most horribly, spiritual death—being cut off from God forever. And everyone must die. You can either die alone or die in Jesus.

In his death Jesus Christ swallowed up our death, and rose again triumphantly to take all of the teeth out of the grave. In the promise of the resurrection, death loses its power. When we die with Jesus, we really live![2]

Sanctification consists of the daily realization that in Christ we have died and in Christ we have been raised. Life change happens as the heart daily grasps death and life. Daily reformation is the fruit of daily resurrection. To get it the other way around (which we always do by default) is to miss the power and point of the gospel. In his book *God in the Dock*, C. S. Lewis makes the obvious point that "you can't get second things by putting them first; you can get second things only by putting first things first."[3] Behavior (good or bad) is a second thing and when we make it a first thing, we resort to the type of rules and regulations that Paul warns about here.

Preachers these days are expected to major in "Christian moral renovation." They are expected to provide a practical to-do list, rather than announce, "It is finished." They are expected to do something other than, more than, placarding before their congregation's eyes Christ's finished work, preaching a full absolution solely on the basis of the complete righteousness of Another. The irony is, of course, that when preachers cave in to this pressure, moral renovation does *not* happen. To focus on how I'm doing, more than on what Christ has done, is Christian narcissism (an oxymoron if I ever heard one)—the poison of self-absorption which undermines the power of the gospel in our lives. Martin Luther noted that "the sin underneath all our sins is the lie of the serpent that we cannot trust the love and grace of Christ and that we must take matters into our own hands."

Moral renovation, in other words, *is* to refocus our eyes away from ourselves to *that* Man's obedience, to *that* Man's cross, to *that* Man's blood—to *that* Man's death and resurrection!

"In *my* place condemned *he* stood, and sealed *my* pardon with *his* blood—hallelujah, what a Savior!"

Learning daily to love this glorious exchange, to lean on its finishedness, and to live under its banner *is* what it means to be morally reformed.

Then Paul exposes further the sheer futility of such rules: "These have indeed an appearance of wisdom in promoting self-made religion and asceticism and severity to the body," he acknowledges, "but they are of *no value* in stopping the indulgence of the flesh" (v. 23). When all's said and done, these various rules and practices, all the rituals and disciplines, all the latest methods and techniques and procedures and approaches in spirituality that everyone's buzzing about—all those things are useless. External conformity like that *can never bring about internal transformation*—ever. Outside cleanup can never achieve inside cleanup. External rule keeping doesn't touch the source of sin or temptation; it doesn't penetrate. The sources of sin, Paul reminds us here, are the desires of the heart. And external rule keeping can't fix that.

In these verses Paul essentially shows us that Old Testament religious practices and pagan religious practices are equally enslaving—one's not any worse than the other. That might be shocking to us. We tend to think that strict adherence to Old Testament religious practices might be a little off, but let's face it: it's not really as bad as the practices of pagan spirituality; that's the really bad stuff. But Paul looks at both through the grid of Christ and sees how they're fundamentally the same. Whether it's an Old Testament ritual or some sort of pagan self-help program, if the focus is on what *you must do* instead of what *Jesus has already done*, it's anti-gospel.

Paul is very explicit in this passage. You can't come away from it without an impression that Paul hates man-made rules and regulations. And he hates them because God hates them.

Since the heart of the human problem is the problem of the human heart, rules and regulations are never the solution. *Jesus is.* Behavior modification cannot change the human heart. You and I need this reminder all the time, and that's why we turn to the gospel.

RESIZED SELF

Paul opens Colossians 3 with an incredible invitation based on gospel reality: "If then you have been raised with Christ, seek the things that are above, where Christ is, seated at the right hand of God. Set your minds on things that are above, not on things that are on earth. For you have died, and your life is hidden with Christ in God" (vv. 1–3). Timothy Keller expresses powerfully the critical importance of these words to our fight against idolatry in light of the gospel:

> Idolatry is not just a failure to obey God, it is a setting of the whole heart on something besides God. This cannot be remedied only by repenting that you have an idol, or using willpower to try to live differently. Turning from idols is not less than those two things, but it is also far more. "Setting the mind and heart on things above" where "your life is hid with Christ in God" (Colossians 3:1–3) means appreciation, rejoicing, and resting in what Jesus has done for you. It entails joyful worship, a sense of God's reality in prayer. Jesus must become more beautiful to your imagination, more attractive to your heart, than your idol. That is what will replace your counterfeit gods. If you uproot the idol and fail to "plant" the love of Christ in its place, the idol will grow back.[4]

Our equation—Jesus plus nothing equals everything—is effectual only when that first word, Jesus, represents someone with the kind of beauty and attractiveness that Keller speaks of, drawing your heart's devotion.

And in the gospel, God has everything to make that exact dynamic a living option for us. As Paul proceeds further in gospel-energized and gospel-motivated teaching in Colossians 3, he speaks about our having "put off the old self with its practices" and having "put on the new self, which is being renewed in knowledge after the image of its creator" (vv. 9–10). His point is that Christianity isn't turning over a new leaf; it's receiving a new life.

The new self Paul speaks of will emerge more and more as we allow the gospel to remove idolatry's shackles. Suddenly, stepping out into the gospel's freedom, we can see ourselves as we really are and not be panic-stricken. We're released from the pressure of having to do and be everything in order to meet our vast unmet inner needs. We finally sense how Jesus is the everything who meets those needs.

The gospel liberates us to be okay with not being okay. We know we're not—though we try very hard to convince other people we are. But the gospel tells us, "Relax, it is finished."

Because of the gospel, we have nothing to prove or protect. We can stop pretending. The gospel frees us from trying to impress people, to prove ourselves to people, to make people think we're something that we're not. The gospel frees us from what one writer calls "the law of capability"—the law, he says, "that judges us wanting if we are not capable, if we cannot handle it all, if we are not competent to balance our diverse commitments without a slip."[5] The gospel grants us the strength to admit we're weak and needy and restless—knowing that Christ's finished work has proven to be all the strength and fulfillment and peace we could ever want, and more.

The gospel frees us from the urge to self-gain, to push our-selves forward for our own purposes and agenda and self-esteem. When you understand that your significance and identity and purpose and direction are all anchored in Christ, you don't have to win—you're free to lose. And nothing in this broken world can beat a person who isn't afraid to lose! You'll be free to say crazy, risky, counterintuitive stuff like, "To live is Christ, and to die is gain" (Phil. 1:21)! That's pure, unadulterated freedom.

Since Jesus is our strength, our weaknesses don't threaten our sense of worth and value. Now we're free to admit our wrongs and weaknesses without feeling as if our flesh is being ripped off our bones.

AVOIDING THE GOSPEL

Since all this is true, have you ever asked yourself, *Why do I avoid the gospel?* Christians avoid the gospel on a daily basis—because that's exactly what sin is. If we're honest, we'll admit that every day we try to avoid the gospel at some level. It's what we do when-ever we as Christians sin. It's a flight from God in thought, word, or deed. And that flight from God always assumes an avoidance of the gospel.

Why do we do this? I'll admit why I do it. It's because the gos-pel makes me disappear. The gospel obliterates me, in a sense. Suddenly life is no longer about my little world and my standards and rules and goals and preferences. It's no longer about me and what I want. It's no longer about my strengths and achievements and attainments.

The gospel erases us, in that sense, which is why we avoid it. But that erasing of self is the key to our freedom.

The gospel doesn't take you deeper into yourself; the gos-pel takes you away from yourself. That's why Paul reminds the Colossians (and us), "You have died, and your life is hidden with

Christ in God" (3:3). The gospel frees us to realize that, while we matter, we're *not the point*.

The gospel frees us from the debilitating frustration of not getting what we think we want, because the gospel shouts to all of us that life isn't about our comfort, our ease, our preferences; it's about God and his glory, his gospel, his church, his way, his kingdom. It's about his Son, Jesus, reigning as king.

Perhaps the biggest difference between the practical effect of sin and the practical effect of the gospel is that sin turns us inward and the gospel turns us outward. The gospel causes us to look up and out, away from ourselves. It turns our gaze upward to God and outward to others, both to those inside the church and to those outside it. The gospel causes us to love God and to love others, which of course is how Jesus summed up the entirety of the law.

We tend to think of good works monastically, individualistically. Many of us think about good works in terms of personal piety, internal devotion, and spiritual disciplines: praying, reading the Bible, going to church, and so on. And while these are all important aspects of Christian living, it's interesting that when James makes his strong point (in James 2:14–26) about faith without works being dead, the works he describes are not works of private spirituality but of public service.

In James 1:27 and 2:15–16, he makes it clear that true spirituality takes us away from ourselves and into the messy lives of other people. True spirituality is not introverted, but extroverted. It doesn't take us deeper into ourselves; it sends us further out. It doesn't make us more introspective but more extrospective— looking outward. In fact, real spiritual growth happens as we look up to Christ and what he did, out to our neighbors and what they need, *not* in to ourselves and how we're doing.

Our natural tendency is to focus on ourselves—on our obedience (or lack thereof), on our performance (good or bad), on our holiness—instead of on Christ and his obedience, his performance, and his holiness for us. We all possess a natural proclivity to turn God's good-news announcement that we've been set free into a narcissistic program of self-improvement. When we do this, we fail to see the needs of our neighbors and serve them. After all, as Martin Luther said, "God doesn't need our good works, but our neighbor does."

My greatest need and yours is to look at Christ more than we look at ourselves. The gospel empowers us to escape our predicament of being curved in on ourselves. In the gospel, God comes after us because *we need him*, not because he needs us. I'm stirred here by Elyse Fitzpatrick's words:

> Whenever the gospel slips from our conscious thought, our religion becomes all about our performance, and then we think everything that happens or will ever happen is about us. When I forget the incarnation, sinless life, death, resurrection, and ascension, I quickly believe that I'm supposed to be the unrivaled, supreme, and matchless one. It's at this point that I'm particularly in need of an intravenous dose of gospel truth. He is preeminent. "For from him and through him and to him are all things. To him be glory forever. Amen" (Rom. 11:36).[6]

Returning to the gospel is a return to reality. Reminded of the gospel, we're reminded that sin enslaves by making us big; the gospel frees by making us small. Our self-esteem culture would have us believe that the bigger we become, the freer we'll be. But the gospel turns that on its head—the smaller we become, the freer we will be. We begin to decrease; Christ begins to increase. The world says the more independent you become, the freer and stronger you'll be; the gospel says the more dependent on God you become, the freer and stronger you'll be.

CREATED AND REDEEMED FOR BEAUTY

God created you for beauty—and redeemed you for beauty—so that you and your joy and peace and gratitude for what he's done for you in Christ would be put on display in a dark, watching world.

The world isn't captivated by people trying to give the impression they have it all together. That's not what draws them. What captures their attention is the sight of humble, desperate, dependent people who acknowledge their sin and who point to their Savior as the only one who can rescue us. The world, in other words, needs our confession, not our competence.

Tragically, moralism is what people most outside the church think we're talking about when we say *gospel* or *Christianity*. That's what enters their minds. Most people inside the church give most people outside the church the impression that Christianity is all about observing certain codes of behavior and abstaining from others. It's all about rules and standards and good behavior and cleaning up your act. We're really good at communicating that to the world.

The only way we'll be able to reach people for Christ is to differentiate legalism from the gospel. From a human standpoint, we have to help them understand that rules and regulations and standards and behavior modification are not the heart of Christianity. We have to show them that the gospel is radically different. We need to somehow make it clear that Jesus came first not to make bad people good, but to make dead people alive; that the primary goal of the gospel is to bring about mortal resurrection, not moral reformation. Christianity is not the move from vice to virtue, but rather the move from virtue to grace.[7] We need to demonstrate and articulate this difference. We need to be able to distinguish between religion (all about my need to do) and the gospel (all about what Jesus has done).

Pascal expressed it well when he said that we should make people wish the gospel were true, then show them that it is. Is your life—is my life—causing the people around us to hope desperately that the gospel is true? Is there a gospel-soaked attractiveness to our lives? Does an aroma of grace spill out from us into selfless service to others?

PART FIVE

EVERYTHING

=

9

EVERYTHING NOW, AND MORE COMING

Jesus plus nothing equals everything—in the blazing light of Christ's divine, overflowing fullness, we've seen how the "nothing" in our equation is so exceedingly empty and void. Now, let's assess just how exceedingly abundant the "everything" can become for us.

GOSPEL HUB

We've recognized that once God rescues sinners, his plan isn't to steer them beyond the gospel but to move them more deeply into it. That's because the gospel isn't the first step in a stairway of truths but more like the hub in a wheel of truth.

After all, the only antidote to sin is the gospel—always has been, always will be. And since Christians remain sinners even after they're converted, the gospel must be the medicine a Christian takes every day. We can think of it this way: since we never leave off sinning, we can never leave off the gospel.

In Romans, Paul calls the gospel "the power of God for salvation to everyone who believes" (1:16), and contrary to what many Christians conclude, he didn't simply mean the power of God unto conversion. The gospel remains the power of God for salvation *until we're glorified.* We need God's rescue every day, in every way, because we are, as John Calvin expressed it, partly unbelievers until we die, for we remain sinners until we die. There's nothing anyone can add to the gospel that can give us more rescue than the gospel alone does. Jesus plus nothing equals everything; everything minus Jesus equals nothing.

We never leave the gospel, ever—even as we move into deeper theological waters. As Tim Keller says, the gospel isn't simply the ABCs of Christianity, but the A to Z of Christianity. All theology is an exposition of the gospel, a further articulation of the gospel in all its facets, meticulously unfolding all its liberating implications and empowering benefits.

And on the practical side, all true maturity and further growth in Christian living is simply the appropriation of the gospel and its benefits in daily life.

And those blessings truly amount to *everything*—to an extent beyond our imagining.

BLESSINGS BIRTHED IN GOD'S PROMISES

The daily reality of the gospel is the reason we can enjoy and revel in the fact that "all the promises of God find their Yes in him"—in Christ (2 Cor. 1:20). Our reborn existence as believers becomes an adventure of embracing these promises more and more as we journey through life. This is something Michael Horton emphasizes in *The Gospel-Driven Life*:

> Christians are driven by God's promises, and directed by God's purposes. . . . Laws, principles, suggestions, and good advice can set our course, but only the gospel promise can fill our sails and restore to us the joy of our salvation.[1]

The apostle Peter richly elaborates on this connection between the *everything* we enjoy and the promises of God:

> His divine power has granted to us *all things* that pertain to
> life and godliness, through the knowledge of him who called
> us to his own glory and excellence, by which he has grant-
> ed to us *his precious and very great promises*, so that through
> them you may become partakers of the divine nature, having
> escaped from the corruption that is in the world because of
> sinful desire. (2 Pet. 1:3–4)

It's *all there* for us—in his promises! *Everything* we need for life
and godliness is there. Remember the sweeping promise of Jesus,
our good shepherd, regarding his sheep? "I came that they may
have life and have it abundantly" (John 10:10).

The quantity of our promised blessings is so great that they're
portrayed as a multiplication in words of prayer and greeting
spoken to believers by various apostles: "May grace and peace be
multiplied to you"; "May grace and peace be *multiplied* to you in
the knowledge of God and of Jesus our Lord"; "May mercy, peace,
and love be *multiplied* to you" (1 Pet. 1:2; 2 Pet. 1:2; Jude 2).

This experience of multiplied blessings is truly what God
has designed for us. Are your eyes open to see it? And when you
do see it, what are the impressions in your mind and heart and
the impact on your life? Are you living your day increasingly
as a grateful recipient of his multiplied everything? Or is there
still a lingering poverty, almost a sense of spiritual cringing and
cowering?

OUR NEW AND EXALTED IDENTITY

Our personal experience of gospel blessings is rooted in the
wonder of our being *in Christ*, the amazing truth that we've seen
Paul emphasize in Colossians. If we're in Christ, then everything
we need, we already possess. By placing our ultimate trust in the
finished work of Christ, all he has secured for sinners becomes
ours. Access to God and affection from God can never be lost;

the extravagant riches of God's pardon and power become ours *in him*.

It also means an exalted, unmatched identity for us. While the world constantly tempts us to locate our identity in something or someone smaller than Jesus, the gospel liberates us by revealing that our true identity is locked in Christ. Our connection in and with Christ is the truest definition of who we are.

When most of us stop long enough to consider what establishes our identity, what really makes us who we are, many of us act as if the answer to this consideration is "our performance." In *Who Will Deliver Us*, Paul Zahl expands on this:

> If I can do enough of the right things, I will have established my worth. Identity is the sum of my achievements. Hence, if I can satisfy the boss, meet the needs of my spouse and children, and still do justice to my inner aspirations, then I will have proven my worth. There are infinite ways to prove our worth along these lines. The basic equation is this: I am what I do. It is a religious position in life because it tries to answer in practical terms the question, Who am I and what is my niche in the universe? On this reading, my niche is in proportion to my deeds. In Christian theology, such a position is called justification by works. It assumes that my worth is measured by my performance. Conversely, it conceals, thinly, a dark and ghastly fear: If I do not perform, I will be judged unworthy. To myself I will cease to exist.[2]

The gospel frees us from this pressure to perform, this slavish demand to "become." The gospel liberatingly declares that in Christ "we already are." If you're a Christian, here's the good news: who you *really* are has nothing to do with you—how much you can accomplish, who you can become, your behavior (good or bad), your strengths, your weaknesses, your sordid past, your family background, your education, your looks, and so on. Your identity is firmly anchored in Christ's accomplishment, not yours; his strength, not yours; his performance, not yours; his victory, not yours. Your identity is steadfastly established in his substitution, not in your sin. As my friend Justin Buzzard recently said, "The gospel doesn't just free you from what other people think about you; it frees you from what you think about yourself." You're free!

Now you can spend your life giving up your place for others instead of guarding it from others, because your identity is in Christ, not in your place. Now you can spend your energy going to the back instead of getting to the front, because your identity is in Christ, not in your position. You can also spend your life giving, not taking, because your identity is in Christ, not in your possessions. All this is our new identity—all because of Christ's finished work declared to us in the gospel.

Paul speaks of our "having been buried with him [with Christ] in baptism," in which we "were also raised with him through faith in the powerful working of God, who raised him from the dead" (Col. 2:12). Our old identity—the things that previously "made us"—has been put to death. Our new identity is "in Christ." We've been raised with Christ to walk "in newness of life"—no longer needing to depend on the "old things" to make us who we are.

When we truly see and understand all these aspects of what we've become in Jesus Christ, what more could we possibly ever want or need in our self-identity? Here in Christ we have worth and purpose and security and significance that make utterly laughable all the transient things of this world that we're so frequently tempted to identify ourselves by.

EVERYTHING, EVERYWHERE IN SCRIPTURE

For seeing the *everythingness* Christ has won for us, we've especially focused on the book of Colossians. But of course this magnitude and comprehensiveness, this vastness and totality of promises and blessings that God makes available for us through the gospel of Christ, is portrayed everywhere in Scripture. The Bible's big picture is not only about the mighty dimensions of who God is and what he does, but also about all that we're given and promised by him through Christ.

When our hearts are tenderized by trust in God through dependence on the gospel, our spiritual eyes are more open to seeing this everywhere. These *vastnesses* we see on the Bible's pages are ultimately beyond our comprehension in their full dimension, but still they're there for a reason, and God wants us to encounter them and reflect on them with recognition and awe.

When we open ourselves to these wonders of abundance and magnitude, we start to see them everywhere in God's Word. We notice, for example, that the *everything* is truly for *everyone* who believes—not just for the super-spiritual. This is why Paul told the Colossians that from Christ "the *whole* body" is nourished and unified and grows "with a growth that is from God" (2:19).

In the new-covenant chapter of Hebrews (chapter 8), God makes the promise regarding his people that "they shall all know me, from the least of them to the greatest" (v. 11).

Paul reiterates how the gospel's wide reach includes all believers in the abundance of fresh blessings: "Therefore, if *anyone* is in Christ, he is a new creation. The old has passed away; behold, the new has come. *All* this is from God, who through Christ reconciled us to himself" (2 Cor. 5:17–18). And he closes his letter to the Ephesians with these words spoken for the benefit and encouragement of every believer: "Grace be with *all* who love our Lord Jesus Christ with love incorruptible" (6:24).

GIVEN AND GOOD, AND OURS FOREVER

In his epistle to the Romans, Paul especially emphasized the *givenness* and goodness and permanence of the everything that's ours in Christ.

In the closing verses of Romans 8, Paul turns our eyes to the *everything* in a passage that, in context, is particularly sensitive to the sufferings we so often experience. But look at how Paul encourages us about the *everything*: "We know that for those who love God *all things* work together for good, for those who are called according to his purpose" (8:28). Paul at once promises that God has predestined and forever assured our calling, our justification, and our glorification; then he asks, "What shall we say to these things?" Some of his longsuffering readers might well be doubting or discouraged; some might fear the loss of certain blessings. But Paul insists: "He who did not spare his own Son but gave him up for us *all*, how will he not also with him graciously give us *all things*?" (vv. 31–32).

Paul mentions the all-too-real ordeals that he and many other believers had faced in those days—"tribulation, or distress, or persecution, or famine, or nakedness, or danger, or sword" (v. 35). Could such things "separate us from the love of Christ?" Paul even throws in an ominous-sounding Old Testament passage: "As it is written, 'For your sake we are being killed all the day long; we are regarded as sheep to be slaughtered.'" That's exactly what it felt like. So, had the fullness of God forsaken them? Paul's voice rings out: "No, in all these things we are more than conquerors through him who loved us" (v. 37). He even spells out an encompassing list of possible and perceived barriers, nullifying each one in order to declare that absolutely *nothing* "in all creation will be able to separate us from the love of God in Christ Jesus our Lord" (vv. 35–39). Nothing whatsoever could ever cut us off from the magnificent comprehensive of the Lord's devoted care and nurture.

His promise of *everything* is for our darkest days as well as for our brightest.

A SPIRIT-GUARDED EVERYTHING

In his first epistle to the Corinthians, Paul stresses the connection of our *everything* with the Spirit as well as with Christ. We learn that the *everything* is Spirit-searched and Spirit-known. Paul characterizes these things as humanly inconceivable: "What no eye has seen, nor ear heard, nor the heart of man imagined"; this, he says, is "what God has prepared for those who love him"; then he adds, "These things God has revealed to us through the Spirit. For the Spirit searches *everything*, even the depths of God" (1 Cor. 2:9–10). Our own *everything* comes out of the mysterious depths of the divine inter-sharing of everything.

Our experience of this multiplies into an incredible dimension of comprehensiveness, something no unbeliever could fathom. Ultimately, Paul says, "The spiritual person judges *all* things, but is himself to be judged by no one" (v. 15)—something made possible because "we have the mind of Christ" (v. 16).

In the context of Paul's rich gospel proclamation and commitment and affirmation in these early chapters of 1 Corinthians, he goes on to declare this: "So let no one boast in men. For *all things* are yours, whether Paul or Apollos or Cephas or the world or life or death or the present or the future—*all* are yours, and you are Christ's, and Christ is God's" (3:21–23). Those last phrases recall Jesus's own words of incredible encouragement spoken to the disciples after his resurrection: "I am ascending to my Father and your Father, to my God and your God" (John 20:17).

Because the Father has embraced the Son and the Son embraces us, we're fully enfolded into the arms of the Father.

This means that for Christians, the level of passion with which God loves you is not determined by the level of passion with which you love him. The Son's passion for you secured the Father's passion for you. *All things are yours*—the *everything* is eternally assured for us because of the gospel that has brought us into the Lord's full familial possession.

Jesus himself had spoken of the Holy Spirit's connection to our experience of the *everything*. He told his disciples, "The Helper, the Holy Spirit, whom the Father will send in my name, he will teach you *all things* and bring to your remembrance *all* that I have said to you" (John 14:26). Later the apostle John would echo that promise in these words written for all believers: "The anointing that you received from him abides in you, and you have no need that anyone should teach you. But as his anointing teaches you about *everything*, and is true, and is no lie—just as it has taught you, abide in him" (1 John 2:27).

It is the Spirit of Christ who daily bears testimony with our spirit that we are "in" forever—that it is finished! It's the Spirit that preaches the gospel to our weary spirits when we need it most, reminding us that everything we need and long for is already ours *in Christ*. It is the Spirit that daily reorients us to the liberating reality that there's nothing left to do. It's done! The Spirit's continuing *subjective work in me* consists of his constant, daily driving me back to Christ's completed *objective work for me*.

DAVID'S EVERYTHING

The sweep of the *everything* throughout the Scriptures encompasses the Old Testament as well. Psalm 16 is a good example, showing us a man who understands the *everything* and its only source. For David says, "You are my Lord; I have *no good* apart from you" (v. 2), and he adds, "I have set the LORD *always* before me" (v. 8). He recognizes the true *nothingness* of idolatry: "The sorrows of those who run after another god shall multiply" (v. 4). He experiences the fullness of promised blessing: "Therefore my heart is glad, and my *whole* being rejoices" (v. 9). And he looks with abundant hope toward a greater experience of the *everything* in the eternal future: "In your presence there is *fullness* of joy; at your right hand are pleasures *forevermore*" (v. 11).

Interestingly, this messianic psalm with its message of fullness is one that Peter quoted in his sermon on the day of Pentecost in Acts 2, as he declared these words to be Christ's experience of the *everything*: "You have made known to me the paths of life; you will make me *full* of gladness with your presence" (v. 28).

Many of David's psalms are flavored by his taste of the *everything* and by his recognitions that these abundant blessings are for all God's people. He breaks forth into song about it: "I will sing to the LORD, because he has dealt *bountifully* with me" (Ps. 13:6). He preaches about it: "Oh, fear the LORD, you his saints, for those who fear him have *no lack!* The young lions suffer want and hunger; but those who seek the LORD *lack no good thing*" (Ps. 34:9–10). And he cries out, "I cry to you, O LORD; I say, 'You are my refuge, *my portion* in the land of the living'" (Ps. 142:5).

THE VAST REACH OF JUSTIFICATION

To close this chapter, let's look briefly at seven biblical words that are particularly associated with the *everything* that's ours in the gospel of Christ.

Our everything means, above all, the miracle of a right standing forever with God. We know this biblically and theologically as *justification*, a big and important and respected word, but we can far too easily miss what it represents and the wonder and awe it deserves. It's a miraculous blessing of the first magnitude.

Oftentimes in our relationship with God, because of sin—our constant tendency to blow it—we think, *I'm ruining my relation-*

ship with God. But I like how one pastor expressed it: "The determining factor in my relationship to God is not my past or my present, but *Christ's* past and *his* present." What an incredibly liberating perspective.

We've spoken before of the great and glorious exchange—Christ's righteousness for our sin—that he accomplished on the cross and which is captured in Paul's statement in 2 Corinthians 5:21 of what God has done: "For our sake he made him to be sin who knew no sin, so that in him we might become the righteousness of God." I like the illustration of the "moral ledger" that Jerry Bridges and Bob Bevington give as they comment on this verse and explain the meaning of justification:

> Imagine there's a moral ledger recording every event of your entire life—all your thoughts, words, actions, even your motives. You might think of it as a mixture of good and bad deeds, with hopefully more good than bad. The Scriptures, however, tell us that even our righteous deeds are unclean in the sight of God (Isaiah 64:6). So Jesus has a perfectly righteous moral ledger, and we have a completely sinful one. However, God took our sins and charged them to Christ, leaving us with a clean sheet. . . .
>
> The word *justified* in Paul's usage means to be counted righteous by God. Even though in ourselves we're completely unrighteous, God counts us as righteous because he has appointed Christ to be our representative and substitute. Therefore when Christ lived a perfect life, in God's sight *we* lived a perfect life. When Christ died on the cross to pay for our sins, *we* died on the cross. . . .
>
> There's an old play on the word *justified*—that it means "just-as-if-I'd never sinned." But here's another way of saying it: "just-as-if-I'd always obeyed." Both are true.[3]

To be justified means that you're forever right with God, eternally *in*.

I once heard a preacher describe justification by using this illustration. Suppose you go out to lunch with a friend, and while you're in the restroom, your friend pays the bill. When you return, your friend says, "We're good." It means your debt has been paid, your obligation taken care of. There's nothing you need to do. When Paul uses the word "justified," he's saying, "You're good; Jesus has paid your debt, your obligation has been paid in full, you owe nothing—you're justified."

Among many other things, this means that God's acceptance of us cannot be gained by our successes nor forfeited by our failures. It means that our standing with God does not depend on our obedience but on Christ's obedience for us. That's the good news; the gospel says it's not what *you must do*, but what *Jesus already did* on behalf of sinners. Our standing with God is not based on our ongoing struggle for Jesus but on Jesus's finished struggle for us.

The gospel is good news—wonderful, positive, invigorating, wholesome, nurturing news—precisely because our relationship to God does not depend on our zeal, our efforts, and our generosity, but on Christ's. That's what makes the gospel such good news. And it's not just good news about how we "get in" initially; it's good news that we go back to every day because we are prone to wander into narcissism (how am I doing? what else do I need to do?). The gospel keeps us fixing our eyes on Jesus, the author and perfecter of our faith. So, the gospel doesn't just justify us; the truth of the gospel sanctifies us and develops us and matures us.

Because of the everlasting truth of our justification, we can "draw near with a true heart in full assurance of faith, with our hearts sprinkled clean from an evil conscience and our bodies washed with pure water" (Heb. 10:22).

FULL FREEDOM

The greatness of our freedom is forever captured in these words of Jesus: "If the Son sets you free, you will be free indeed" (John

8:36). The Son has indeed set us free. Through Christ, God "has delivered us" (Col. 1:13).

Real slavery is living your life trying to gain favor; real freedom is knowing you already have favor—the difference is huge. The gospel frees us to work and live from the secure basis of faith, not fear. We obey from the secure basis of grace, not guilt. And nothing could be more liberating. It means we're no longer enslaved to the arbitrary rules and regulations imposed on us by society, by religious people, and by ourselves. "For *freedom* Christ has set us free," Paul says; "stand firm therefore, and do not submit again to a yoke of slavery" (Gal. 5:1).

As I mentioned earlier, in 2009 it was so important for me to grasp once again that this freedom Jesus secured for me is not freedom *from* pain and suffering; rather, it's a freedom *in* pain and suffering. In our day when the health-and-wealth gospel is preached, it's so critical for Bible-believing, gospel-soaked Christians to understand that nowhere in the Bible does God promise us freedom from our pain and suffering here and now. Rather, the freedom he promises is the freedom not to be enslaved by our pain and suffering while we rest in the assurance that full deliverance from all pain and suffering is coming when Christ returns.

God helped me realize that the kind of freedom he offers in Christ, here and now, is one that we can actually celebrate in times of great trial. And he allowed me to see that since everything I need I already have in Christ, I can spend my life dying. Because Christ is my life, I'm free to die—and free to give everything I have, because in Christ I already have everything I need and can never lose it.

There's no freer place to be in life than going on with Christ, with the one who is himself our true liberty.

And that's exactly what the world needs to see in the church—that we're free people, liberated from every form of bondage.

Keep this in mind: the world isn't scandalized by our freedom but by our fakeness.

GRACE AND PEACE

The essence of what the gospel brings to us can be summed up in the words *grace* and *peace*—the very words Paul uses together in the opening of every single one of his letters, because Paul was a gospel-intoxicated man.

Grace is the root of the gospel; *peace* is the fruit of the gospel. As he did throughout his letters, Paul chose these words carefully and intentionally. Though the phrase "grace and peace to you" might look at first glance like nothing more than an opening salutation, Paul was communicating something very specific and intentional.

At the root of the gospel, the measurelessness of God's grace for us in Christ is clearly stressed in Scripture, along with its incredible power.

"From his fullness we have all received, *grace upon grace*," John tells us (John 1:16). And Paul says, "*Much more* have the grace of God and the free gift by the grace of that one man Jesus Christ *abounded* for *many*" (Rom. 5:15). It's the nature of grace to abound—in quantity as well as effect.

Paul proclaims how "the word of [God's] *grace* . . . is able to build you up and to give you the inheritance among all those who are sanctified" (Acts 20:32). He tells us that "God is able to make *all grace* abound to you, so that having *all sufficiency* in *all things* at *all times*, you may *abound* in *every* good work" (2 Cor. 9:8). And Paul passes along to us a powerful word from the Lord at a point of struggle in his life: "He said to me, '*My grace is sufficient for you*, for my power is made perfect in weakness'" (2 Cor. 12:9). There's no power in the world like the power of grace.

The operation of God's grace on our behalf doesn't imply

any lessening of his demands. God has always and will always demand perfect obedience. But his grace is experienced when we realize that those demands for perfection for each of us have already been met by our Savior, Jesus. Jesus fulfilled all of God's conditions on our behalf so that our relationship with God could be unconditional. Christianity is the only faith system where God both makes the demands and meets them.

Let me share a concern I have. There's a lot of talk about "cross centeredness," as if the death of Christ (what theologians have called "his passive obedience") is more important than the life of Christ (what theologians have called "his active obedience"). The truth is, however, that our redemption depends not only on Christ's substitutionary death but also on his substitutionary life.

J. Gresham Machen's last recorded words (sent by telegram to his friend and colleague John Murray) were these: "So thankful for Christ's active obedience; no hope without it!" He understood that apart from Christ's law-fulfilling life, there's *no* righteousness to impute, and we're therefore left dressed in our own filthy rags.

In his excellent book *Redemption Accomplished and Applied*, John Murray writes:

> The real use and purpose of the formula (active and passive obedience) is to emphasize the two distinct aspects of our Lord's vicarious obedience. The truth expressed rests upon the recognition that the law of God has both penal sanctions and positive demands. It demands not only the full discharge of its precepts but also the infliction of penalty for all infractions and shortcomings. It is this twofold demand of the law of God which is taken into account when we speak of the active and passive obedience of Christ. Christ as the vicar of his people came under the curse and condemnation due to sin and he also fulfilled the law of God in all its positive requirements. In other words, he took care of the guilt of sin and perfectly fulfilled the demands of righteousness. He perfectly met both the penal and the preceptive requirements of God's law. The

passive obedience refers to the former and the active obedience to the latter. [4]

Christ's life, in other words, is just as central to our rescue as his death. We are not saved apart from the law. Rather, we are saved *in Christ*, who perfectly kept the law on our behalf. After all, Christ himself said that he had come "not to abolish the law but to fulfill it"—not for himself, but for us. Michael Horton points this out in his excellent essay "Obedience Is Better Than Sacrifice":

> As important as it is that Christ bore the penalty of our sins on the cross, it is just as important that he triumphed over the powers of evil and recapitulated the history of fallen humanity and Israel. Adam was commanded to obey God's law and failed, Israel was commanded to obey God's law and failed, but Christ came into this world and completed a life of perfect obedience to the law of his Father. Christ the righteous One was indeed the Last Adam, the True Israel. . . . We have not only been forgiven on the basis of Christ's curse-bearing death, but justified on the basis of his probation-fulfilling life. [5]

This is nothing new. It's been a stamp of historic theological conviction for centuries, as the Heidelberg Catechism's question 60 shows:

> God imputes to me the perfect satisfaction, righteousness, and holiness of Christ, as if I had never committed any sin, and myself had accomplished all the obedience which Christ has rendered for me.

So, Christ's death is *not* the center of the gospel any more than his life is the center of the gospel. One without the other fails to bring about redemption. It's much more theologically accurate to say that *Christ himself* is the center of the gospel. He lived the life we couldn't live and died the death we should have died.

And this happens all of grace.

If this grace is the root of the gospel, then peace is the gospel's fruit. "Therefore, since we have been justified by faith, we have peace with God through our Lord Jesus Christ" (Rom. 5:1). Here is genuine peace, and it's built on a real change in status before God—from standing guilty before God the judge to standing righteous before God our Father. This is the objective custody of even the weakest believer. It's a peace that rests squarely on the fact that we've already been "reconciled to God by the death of his Son" (v. 10), justified before God once and for all through faith in Christ's finished work. It will surely produce real feelings and robust action, but this peace with God that Paul describes rests securely on the work of Christ for us, outside us. The more I look into my own heart for peace, the less I find. On the other hand, the more I look to Christ and his promises for peace, the more I find.

The word Paul uses for peace, *shalom*, means more than merely the absence of conflict; it means fullness and wholeness and completeness. It carries with it a sense of things being settled. The peace that the Bible has in view is a harmony, a serenity, a tranquility coming only from God's rescuing grace. Nothing and no one in this world can provide this deep, abiding sense of *okayness* except the peace of God extended to us through the gospel. As Isaiah says, "The effect of righteousness will be peace, and the result of righteousness, quietness and trust forever" (Isa. 32:17).

This quiet confidence is what my grandmother referred to as a quiet knowing—that deep, abiding sense of wholeness, completeness, and calmness; that regardless of what is happening in our life and world, regardless of the tragedy we may be facing, there's a peace of God that transcends all understanding, going deep into the fabric of our being. It's the fruit of what Christ came to accomplish for sinners like you and me; when God has made peace with us, when things between us and God have been settled because of Christ's work, we experience a settled assurance about our life that was impossible to know before.

The words of Psalm 116:7 could serve as a summary of the peace we're invited to as a result of the gospel of Christ: "Return, O my soul, to your rest; for the LORD has dealt *bountifully* with you."

A GROWING HOPE

Paul speaks in Colossians of "the hope laid up for you in heaven" (1:5). It's a hope so vast that all earth can't contain it.

The *everythingness* of Christ means we can "have the full assurance of hope until the end" (Heb. 6:11). It looks to the future, and yet it can be experienced now, in increasing dimension in our daily experience, as Peter tells us: "Set your hope *fully* on the grace that will be brought to you at the revelation of Jesus Christ" (1 Pet. 1:13).

This is the hope. Paul explains more about it in 2 Corinthians 4:16–18: "So we do not lose heart. Though our outer self is wasting away, our inner self is being renewed day by day. For this light momentary affliction is preparing for us an eternal weight of glory beyond all comparison, as we look not to the things that are seen but to the things that are unseen. For the things that are seen are transient, but the things that are unseen are eternal." These words come from a man who has suffered greatly for the cause of Christ, but who never lost hope.

How easy it is to lose sight of the benefits that we have in Christ as we go through life's trials. It's easy to do because of the *not-yetness* of our promised blessings, the full experience of our freedom and peace. The Bible makes it clear that as Christians we've already been saved from sin's penalty, and we're currently being saved from sin's power; but our being saved from the presence of sin altogether will happen one day when Jesus comes back. We've already been truly saved but not yet fully saved.

But our fullness of hope allows us *now* to have full and confident expectation of all that is coming to us in the end. For the Christian, the best is yet to come.

GREAT JOY

"These things I have spoken to you," Jesus says, "that my joy may be in you, and that your joy may be full" (John 15:11). Like every other blessing in the Christian life, our joy comes because of our union with Christ, and that's what allows it to be experienced to the full.

Our joy is indescribably glorious in its fullness. In the opening lines of his first epistle, Peter points us to Christ in the face of our fiery trials, and he writes, "Though you have not seen him, you love him. Though you do not now see him, you believe in him and rejoice with joy that is inexpressible and *filled with glory*" (1:8).

Jesus also linked our fullness of joy to our prayerful relationship with him: "Ask, and you will receive, that your *joy may be full*" (John 16:24).

This gospel joy is exactly what was announced by the angel in the skies near Bethlehem, at the hour of Christ's incarnation: "Fear not, for behold, I bring you good news of *great joy* that will be for all the people" (Luke 2:10).

DEEP, DEEP LOVE

We've seen already the magnitude of God's love for us in Christ as proclaimed so profoundly by Paul at the end of Romans 8, as he concludes that absolutely nothing "in all creation will be able to separate us from the love of God in Christ Jesus our Lord" (v. 39).

In praise to the Lord, David proclaims, "Your steadfast love is *great to the heavens*" (Ps. 57:10). And David takes it personally, and in a gospel sense: "For *great* is your steadfast love toward me; you have delivered my soul from the depths of Sheol" (Ps. 86:13). He knows that the extent of this love can be experienced by all God's people: "For as high as the heavens are above the earth, *so great* is his steadfast love toward those who fear him" (Ps. 103:11).

The Psalms go on to emphatically assure us that this heaven-reaching love for us will never end: "His steadfast love endures *forever*" is the line repeated twenty-six times in Psalm 136.

Nowhere else is this love seen for all its incredible immensity than in the gospel. Paul articulates it in a passage I hope that you'll memorize (if you haven't already) and treasure forever in your heart:

> But God, being *rich in mercy*, because of the *great love* with which he loved us, even when we were dead in our trespasses, made us alive together with Christ—by grace you have been saved—and raised us up with him and seated us with him in the heavenly places in Christ Jesus, so that in the coming ages he might show the *immeasurable riches* of his grace in kindness toward us in Christ Jesus. (Eph. 2:4–7)

Of all the aspects of our *everything*, it's this vast love of God as shown to us in Christ that seems to have captivated most the hearts and imaginations of hymn writers and songwriters down through the ages. This is just one selection, among many, that conveys beautifully the *everything* of this love:

> O the deep, deep love of Jesus,
> Vast, unmeasured, boundless, free,
> Rolling as a mighty ocean
> In its fullness over me.
> Underneath me, all around me,
> Is the current of Thy love;
> Leading onward, leading homeward

To my glorious rest above.

O the deep, deep love of Jesus—
Spread His praise from shore to shore!
How He loveth, ever loveth,
Changeth never, nevermore;
How He watches o'er His loved ones,
Died to call them all His own;
How for them He intercedeth,
Watcheth o'er them from the throne.

O the deep, deep love of Jesus
Love of ev'ry love the best!
'Tis an ocean vast of blessing;
'Tis a haven sweet of rest.
O the deep, deep love of Jesus—
'Tis a heav'n of heav'ns to me;
And it lifts me up to glory
For it lifts me up to Thee.[6]

MISSING ANYTHING?

Justification, freedom, grace, peace, hope, joy, love—and there
are a great many other biblical words whose part in our *everything*
we could also explore. There's *forgiveness, wisdom, comfort,* and
strength, to name just a few.

In Christ we have so very much. There's so very much, and no
chapter or book could ever begin to describe it adequately.

A few days before his crucifixion, Jesus reminded his disciples of a mission trip he'd sent them on. Jesus asked them, "When
I sent you out with no moneybag or knapsack or sandals, did you
lack *anything?*" Then he answered, "Nothing" (Luke 22:35).

Perhaps somewhere in the course of eternity, our Lord will
ask us the same question about our experience here: "Did you
lack anything?" And we'll be fully able to answer, "No, nothing
was ever lacking. You gave us everything for our identity, you

gave us everything for our peace and security, everything for our freedom, everything for our hope, everything for our justification before God, and all love and joy, all from your abundant grace. And so we came to understand that all this and more is what *You plus nothing* equals. That's what we discovered."

Then we'll be able to add, with praise and gratitude, "Yes, Lord, you were our good shepherd—we never lacked. Our cup overflowed. Surely goodness and mercy followed us *all the days of our lives*—and now we shall dwell in your house forever."

Then we'll see just how right Paul was when he promised, "My God will supply *every* need of yours according to his riches in glory in Christ Jesus" (Phil. 4:19).

10

OUR FULL RESPONSE

In the first chapter of Colossians there's a quite interesting verse that some have stumbled over. The context is the following passage, in which Paul speaks of what God has done through Christ for sinners. See if you can spot the troublesome phrase:

> And you, who once were alienated and hostile in mind, doing evil deeds, he has now reconciled in his body of flesh by his death, in order to present you holy and blameless and above reproach before him, if indeed you continue in the faith, stable and steadfast, not shifting from the hope of the gospel that you heard, which has been proclaimed in all creation under heaven, and of which I, Paul, became a minister. (vv. 21–23)

You probably saw it at once. It's the phrase in the middle of that paragraph, beginning with the words "if indeed you continue in the faith . . ." At first glance, some have thought Paul is saying by this statement that we can experience the reconciliation that's mentioned only conditionally, by complete faithfulness and firmness in our Christian walk.

However, the grammatical mood of the particular Greek wording here tells us something else, as Bible teachers and commentaries point out. As one leading study Bible explains it, the grammatical form "indicates that Paul fully expects that the Colossian believers will continue in the faith; no doubt is expressed."[1] Paul in these words is actually *assuring* the Colossian believers that because they've been reconciled through Christ's work on their behalf, therefore they'll indeed continue in the faith, stable and steadfast. Spiritual steadfastness and stability will become a growing experience in their life. Paul isn't saying that our performance leads to our rescue; he's saying that genuine rescue leads to our performance. Our improvement comes from God's approval; God's approval doesn't come from our improvement.

Here in these early chapters of Colossians, where gospel indicatives and gospel declarations are paramount, we also see Paul blending in an implication of the kind of imperatives that appropriately flow from gospel truths.

In fact, the same thing is observed in Paul's prayer for the Colossians even earlier in this opening chapter, where he asks God to fill them with full spiritual apprehension of his will, so they can "walk in a manner worthy of the Lord, fully pleasing to him, bearing fruit in every good work" (v. 10). Clearly, the liberating truths of the gospel are meant to lead us to a liberated life of action, of stepping forth in faith and doing the good works he directs and enables us to do.

Paul's words in Colossians 1:23 about continuing in the faith, stable and steadfast, are a reminder to us that our Christian walk isn't meant to be characterized by feebleness and shakiness, much less by doubt, distrust, and defiance. Thankfully, the gospel makes it possible for us to avoid all that.

Paul is talking here about the great Christian doctrine of the perseverance of the saints—that once God saves us, we will persevere to the end *because* Jesus persevered for us to the end.

WHAT THIS IS NOT ABOUT

As we continue working out our life of obedience in light of Christ's obedience, one thing is clear: the issue is never *whether or not to obey*. We know the Bible has plenty to say about keeping

God's commands. That's indisputable. But what motivates our obedience, what animates our obedience, and what prompts us to obey? Is it fear or faith? Is it guilt or gratitude?

Paul says that when we divorce obligations from gospel declarations, then our obedience becomes nothing more than behavioral compliance to rules without heart change. But when God's amazing grace in the gospel grips our hearts, the motivational structure of our hearts is radically changed, and we begin to obey out of faith not fear, gratitude not guilt.

When I begin analyzing and evaluating my own heart and the motivations behind what I do, I begin to discover a lot of moralistic tendencies. That's why, as I've said so often, we need to be making a beeline for the finished work of Christ every day, because only the gospel can crush the moralistic tendencies that are the natural default mode of our hearts.

WHY DO RIGHT?

As you pursue that kind of self-evaluation, think about this question: Why should we do the right thing?

Most of us would automatically answer, "Because it's the right thing to do." But that's not the thrust of what the Bible says. The Bible *does* tell us that we're to do what is right, but it emphasizes the reason: because in Christ, God has done you right. Ephesians 4:32 is a good example: "Be kind to one another, tenderhearted, forgiving one another, *as God in Christ forgave you.*"

Another is 1 John 3:16: "By this we know love, that *he laid down his life for us*, and we ought to lay down our lives for the brothers."

It's always the gospel of God's free grace that should motivate our right doing; otherwise we're nothing better than Pharisees, making sure we're keeping all the rules, mainly because when we do, we feel better about ourselves—especially when we compare ourselves to those who aren't doing right.

These examples are all over the Bible. You'll never find an obligation that isn't closely associated, in its context, with a gospel declaration. The Bible never starts with what we need to do; it always begins with what God has already done. To get it the other way around makes Christianity just another self-help program, just another curriculum of self-improvement. Self-improvement for the sake of self-improvement is *not* the gospel; it's *not* biblical Christianity. And yet so many people, both inside and outside the church, think that's what Christianity is all about. Jesus or no Jesus, we just want everything to be clean and safe. Jesus or no Jesus, we just want our kids to behave and to achieve. Jesus or no Jesus, we just want our marriage to be easy and personally fulfilling.

Most of us become guilty of this Christless Christianity because we look at the Bible and we see all of the imperatives without first being washed by the indicatives. We spend more time asking what would Jesus do instead of what *did* Jesus do.

We have to keep reminding ourselves of the difference between moralism and the gospel. We have to keep remembering that the reason Christ came was first of all not to make bad people good but to make dead people alive. If we forget that, our Christianity will turn out to be Christless.

WALKING IN STRENGTH

In the second chapter of Colossians, we can see plenty more evidence of the juxtaposition of the gospel and the Christian's obedient walk, and the priority given to the gospel. Colossians 2:6–7 is a prime example here: "Therefore, as you received Christ Jesus the Lord, so *walk* in him, rooted and built up in him and established in the faith, just as you were taught, abounding in thanksgiving." Let's reflect on those verses more closely.

When Paul says in verse 6, "as you received Christ Jesus the Lord," he's not talking here simply about conversion, though that's the way we tend to use the phrase. Paul's meaning is much deeper. He means, *You already received Christ and all the benefits he secured for you.* Christ has secured grace for your past, grace for your present, and grace for your future, and you've already received those benefits in him; it's a done deal. The tense of the verb here is past perfect. That means it's finished.

And because it's finished, everything Christ came to accomplish on behalf of sinners—earning the approval and acceptance of God, earning the affection of God for us, earning access to God on our behalf—all those things we've now received in Christ, so that all that is Christ's becomes ours.

Only after he makes that huge point does Paul say, "Therefore walk in him." Notice, he doesn't say "walk *to* him"—as if we were on our own, separated from him and needing somehow to get to him by way of our own obedience. He says we're to *walk in him*—to walk in Christ, in his strength. Christ is big enough, wide enough, long enough, solid enough to be your path for now and eternity—your lifelong road and everlasting highway. We walk because he came to us, not in order to get to him.

And in verse 7, when Paul says, "rooted and built up in him and established in the faith," that phrase could be literally translated as "having taken root and now getting built up, having been established in the faith." The words for *rooted* and *established* are in the past-perfect Greek tense, while *built up* is present-perfect.

Paul is saying this to the Colossian believers: *Christ has already rooted you, and already established you—and as a result he's currently growing you.* Paul is preaching the gospel to these Christians, reminding them of what has *already* taken place and of what *will* inevitably take place, all because of what Jesus did for them (not what they did for Jesus). He's reminding them of who they are in Christ.

We can "walk in him" because we're *rooted* in him. If you

imagine yourself as being like a tree sending down roots, then Christ is like all the earth, so vast that your roots can always go deeper and stretch out further.

And we're being built up in him, having been established in him—he's the foundation for everything in our lives, the solidifier of everything in our destiny. Calvin comments this way: "The stability of those who rely upon Christ is immovable, and their course is not at all wavering, or liable to error."[2]

Christ's everything for us means our continual growth—our continually being built up and abounding in him—to "grow every day more and more," in Calvin's phrase.[3]

One of the reasons we experience so much failure in the Christian life is that we think more about obligations then we do gospel declarations. We focus on the imperatives, but we pass over the indicatives. We fail in our doing because we fail to grasp first what Christ has already done. This leaves us powerless—running on our own steam. Only when you realize that the gospel has nothing to do with your obedience but with Christ's obedience for you, will you start to obey. The only Christians who end up getting better are those who realize that if they don't get better, God will love them anyway.

Think, for example, of how Paul teaches the Corinthians about generosity in their giving. He doesn't motivate them with guilt, remarking on how selfish they seem to be. Instead he builds his remarks around this point: "For you know the grace of our Lord Jesus Christ, that though he was rich, yet for your sake he became poor, so that you by his poverty might become rich" (2 Cor. 8:9). He's reorienting them to the gospel. He first grips the heart with gospel truth; he doesn't just press the will.

Or notice a single verse in which Paul teaches the Galatians to avoid selfishness and living for the flesh and instead to practice love and servanthood. He says, "For you were called to freedom, brothers. Only do not use your freedom as an opportunity for the flesh, but through love serve one another" (Gal. 5:13). The first part of that verse is a gospel declaration, a gospel indicative. *You were called*—it's a done deal—*to freedom*. You're no longer a slave to sin, no longer a slave to lesser things. It's only after Paul reminds them of the gospel that he gives his command.

GOSPEL LIVELINESS

I have to say that my life has been turned upside-down because of coming to a greater understanding of this truth: the obligations of God's law are always grounded in declarations of God's gospel. And those declarations point immediately to experiencing the realities of the most fruitful life possible.

Hardly any passage in Scripture is more insistent about avoiding sin than Romans 6. But for making that happen, the picture we're given in Romans 6 is not about self-discipline or willpower or law keeping, but about *life*—aliveness, newness, and fruit bearing, all in the Spirit. Sin will have *no* dominion. Read this passage in a fresh way, noticing the preponderance of positive images here:

> What shall we say then? Are we to continue in sin that grace may abound? By no means! How can we who died to sin still live in it? Do you not know that all of us who have been baptized into Christ Jesus were baptized into his death? We were buried therefore with him by baptism into death, in order that, *just as Christ was raised from the dead* by the glory of the Father, *we too might walk in newness of life*. For if we have been united with him in a death like his, we shall certainly be *united with him in a resurrection like his*. We know that our old self was crucified with him in order that the body of sin might be brought to nothing, so that we would no longer be enslaved to sin. For one who has died has been *set free from sin*. Now if we have died with Christ, we believe that *we will also live with him*. We know that Christ, being *raised from the dead*, will never die again; death no longer has dominion

over him. For the death he died he died to sin, once for all, but *the life he lives he lives to God.* So you also must consider yourselves dead to sin and *alive to God in Christ Jesus.* Let not sin therefore reign in your mortal body, to make you obey its passions. Do not present your members to sin as instruments for unrighteousness, but present yourselves to God as those who have been brought from death to *life,* and your members to God as *instruments for righteousness.* For sin will have no dominion over you, since you are not under law but *under grace.* (Rom. 6:1–14)

All this is involved in living according to "the *new way* of the Spirit" that Paul goes on to speak of in Romans 7:6.

IN LIGHT OF THE EVERYTHING

In the last half of Colossians (after emphasizing gospel imperatives in the first two chapters), Paul will go on to pass along plenty of authoritative commands for our behavior and lifestyle and attitudes and relationships.

But notice how he launches into this at the beginning of chapter 3. He doesn't say, *Do these things, or else God will be angry with you.* Rather, he keeps reminding them again of who they now are as a new creation in Christ: "raised with Christ" (v. 1); and having their life "hidden with Christ in God" (v. 3); and having "put on the new self" (v. 10); and now "God's chosen ones, holy and beloved" (v. 12). It's on that basis that he asks them to "put to death therefore what is earthly in you" (v. 5), and to "put on then" the Christlike, Spirit-enabled qualities of "kindness, humility, meekness, and patience" and more (vv. 12–17).

Everything Paul goes on to say, everything he exhorts Christians to do in chapters 3 and 4, he exhorts them to do in light of what he's explained to them—and continues to remind them of—regarding what Christ has already accomplished on their behalf.

EVERYTHING FOR EVERYTHING

Embracing the everything that Christ brings us in the gospel, we're free to give our own everything. That's the freeing factor behind our obedience, an obedience that keeps expanding and intensifying—fueled by grace. Paul tells us, "Therefore, my beloved brothers, be steadfast, immovable, *always abounding* in the work of the Lord, knowing that in the Lord your labor is not in vain" (1 Cor. 15:58).

Paul's words in 1 Thessalonians 5:14–22 are especially reflective of the fullness of our obedient response to the fullness of gospel grace. Notice the words Paul uses:

> We urge you, brothers, admonish the idle, encourage the fainthearted, help the weak, be patient with them *all*. See that *no one* repays anyone evil for evil, but *always* seek to do good to one another and to *everyone*. Rejoice *always*, pray *without ceasing*, give thanks in *all* circumstances; for this is the will of God in Christ Jesus for you. Do not quench the Spirit. Do not despise prophecies, but test *everything*; hold fast what is good. *Abstain* from *every* form of evil.

And then this concluding prayer:

> Now may the God of peace himself sanctify you *completely*, and may your *whole* spirit and soul and body be kept blameless at the coming of our Lord Jesus Christ. (v. 23)

To us, the kind of wholehearted, full-life response that was characteristic of Paul's own life may seem possible only for super-saints. But the overarching point, in light of the gospel, is that giving *our* all in this way is made possible only by receiving and recognizing *his* all.

Consider, for instance, the "good shepherd" passage in John 10 and how often Jesus speaks of laying down his life. Christ has given his all—freeing us to now give our all:

> I am the good shepherd. The good shepherd *lays down his life* for the sheep. I am the good shepherd. I know my own and my own know me, just as the Father knows me and I know the Father; and I *lay down my life* for the sheep. . . . For this reason the Father loves me, because I *lay down my life* that I may take it up again. . . . No one takes it from me, but I *lay it down* of my own accord. I have authority to *lay it down*, and I have authority to take it up again. This charge I have received from my Father. (John 10:11–18)

His sacrifice precedes, animates, and empowers ours. We love him because he first loved us. We're now free to let go of lesser things because he first let go of higher things (Phil. 2:6–8). This is why Paul could say, "I've been found by someone who's worth letting go of everything else for—everything." There's absolutely no way we can live such a life of radical sacrifice—a life of courageous self-giving—apart from the gospel.

I frequently go back to this passage:

> Whatever were gains to me I now consider loss for the sake of Christ. What is more, I consider everything a loss because of the surpassing worth of knowing Christ Jesus my Lord, for whose sake I have lost all things. I consider them garbage, that I may gain Christ and be found in him, not having a righteousness of my own that comes from the law, but that which is through faith in Christ—the righteousness that comes from God on the basis of faith. (Phil. 3:7–9 NIV)

Paul says a lot in those verses. But his main point is that no social or religious achievement, no educational success, no position, no familial heritage, no amount of societal approval is worth holding on to and building your life on, compared to the surpassing worth of knowing Jesus, for whose sake it's worth losing all that you have. Paul considered his "everything" nothing in comparison to the everything of Jesus. For Paul, Jesus plus nothing equals everything; everything minus Jesus equals nothing. That's why, for Paul, giving up everything for Christ was nothing.

WILLING TO SUFFER

It was this realization, that in Christ he already had everything he needed, that gave him his remarkable perspective on suffering:

> Now I rejoice in my sufferings for your sake, and in my flesh I am *filling up* what is lacking in Christ's afflictions for the sake of his body, that is, the church, of which I became a minister according to the stewardship from God that was given to me for you, to make the word of God *fully* known. (Col. 1:24–25)

That first line is a hard statement to understand: "in my flesh I am filling up what is lacking in Christ's afflictions for the sake of his body, that is, the church." At first glance it seems to indicate the insufficiency of Jesus's work on the cross—that we must add our own sufferings to what Jesus did to make up for "what is lacking." But if that's what this verse is saying, it would contradict everything Paul has said up until this point in Colossians, as well as contradict the rest of the Bible.

So what does that verse mean? If it doesn't imply a deficiency in Christ's death, what is Paul talking about? His statement means simply this: when we suffer for Jesus (and all believers do, in some way), we put on display the way Jesus loved and suffered for the world, and so in our own sufferings we extend his sufferings to the world. God intends for Christ's afflictions, his hurt and pain, to be presented to the world through the afflictions of his people. We demonstrate for the watching world his magnificent sufficiency, and we show the world how valuable he is as we partner with him and his sufferings in this way.

That's how we show the world how valuable Jesus is. We're saying, "I've given my life for this; I'm willing to suffer and die for this, because there's nothing in this world more valuable than

Jesus. And I won't hold on to anything in this world if it requires me to loosen my grip on Christ." To suffer well might be the most important sermon we ever preach. It's not that we're unrealistic; we don't ignore suffering, and we feel its pain. But we're able to do this with an internal smile of confident joy.

JOSEPH'S STORY

A few decades ago, at a conference for itinerant evangelists in Amsterdam sponsored by my grandfather, one of the men attending (and who was able to personally meet my grandfather there) was a Maasai warrior from Africa named Joseph. Listen to his story of suffering (as retold by Michael Card):

> One day Joseph, who was walking along one of these hot, dirty African roads, met someone who shared the gospel of Jesus Christ with him. Then and there he accepted Jesus as his Lord and Savior. The power of the Spirit began transforming his life; he was filled with such excitement and joy that the first thing he wanted to do was return to his own village and share that same Good News with the members of his local tribe.
>
> Joseph began going from door-to-door, telling everyone he met about the Cross [suffering!] of Jesus and the salvation it offered, expecting to see their faces light up the way his had. To his amazement the villagers not only didn't care, they became violent. The men of the village seized him and held him to the ground while the women beat him with strands of barbed wire. He was dragged from the village and left to die alone in the bush.
>
> Joseph somehow managed to crawl to a water hole, and there, after days of passing in and out of consciousness, found the strength to get up. He wondered about the hostile reception he had received from people he had known all his life. He decided he must have left something out or told the story of Jesus incorrectly. After rehearsing the message he had first heard, he decided to go back and share his faith once more.

Joseph limped into the circle of huts and began to proclaim Jesus. "He died for you, so that you might find forgiveness and come to know the living God," he pleaded. Again
he was grabbed by the men of the village and held while the
women beat him, reopening wounds that had just begun to
heal. Once more they dragged him unconscious from the village and left him to die.

To have survived the first beating was truly remarkable.
To live through the second was a miracle. Again, days later,
Joseph awoke in the wilderness, bruised, scarred—and deter-
mined to go back.

He returned to the small village and this time, they attacked him before he had a chance to open his mouth. As they
flogged him for the third and probably the last time, he again
spoke to them of Jesus Christ, the Lord. Before he passed out,
the last thing he saw was that the women who were beating
him began to weep.

This time he awoke in his own bed. The ones who had so
severely beaten him were now trying to save his life and nurse
him back to health. The entire village had come to Christ.[4]

That story perfectly illustrates what Paul meant when he
spoke of completing what is lacking in Christ's afflictions for the
sake of his body. You and I will likely never suffer to the physical
extent that Joseph did. But we can be grateful that God uses such
suffering among his people to seal his truth, to showcase his
value, and to make the sufficiency of Christ known to the world.

EXPENDABLE

When gospel grace grips your heart, life becomes all about gospel
grace. When the gospel reorients how you think and feel and live,
all of life becomes about the work Jesus accomplished for us, not
what we can accomplish for him—or anyone else for that matter.
We're liberatingly decreased while Christ is gloriously increased.

Because of this newfound freedom, we suddenly discover

how expendable we really are. I know none of us likes to believe we're expendable, but we are—every single one of us. The world will go on without you; the world will go on without me.

But only the gospel can cause you to rejoice and be glad in your expendability—because the gospel shows us that while we matter, we're not the point. That's liberating, because when we become the hero of our own story, life becomes a tragedy.

Because Jesus was someone, we're free to be no one. Because Jesus was extraordinary, we're free to be ordinary.

Real slavery is self-reliance, self-dependence. Real slavery is a life spent trying to become someone. But the gospel comes in and says we already have in Christ all that we crave, so we're free to live a life of sacrifice, courageously and boldly.

When "Jesus plus nothing equals everything" becomes your way of life, and not just a phrase you like, only then will you experience the freedom and fulfillment you were rescued by God to experience.

11

IN THE NOW

I'm always amazed at how hard it is for my heart to embrace what my head affirms. Everything we've looked at together in this book I easily affirm with every part of my brain. I believe with all my mind that Jesus plus nothing equals everything and that everything minus Jesus equals nothing. I agree with everything we've observed in these pages regarding what the Bible teaches us about Jesus and about our sin and about God's grace and about the gospel.

My belief and conviction in these things has been wonderfully strengthened in the past couple of years. God, by his grace, has enabled me to rediscover the richness of the gospel. In a very difficult period of my life, that rediscovery helped me understand—in bigger, better, deeper ways—what it really means to be approved by God, accepted by God, redeemed by God, forgiven by God, and transferred from darkness to light by God.

The problem is, when I examine my heart honestly, I find many other things smaller than Jesus that I depend on, on a daily basis, to make life go. And I'm sure that's true for you as well—it's an ongoing struggle to embrace and to love with our heart what our mind affirms.

I can say for example, with great conviction, that in Jesus I'm forever accepted and approved by God. I know the Bible teaches that, and I believe the Bible's true. Yet I have to admit that most of the time, approval and acceptance from others seems more tangible, more vivid, more affecting than the abstract notion of God's approval.

It's one thing to affirm the gospel; it's something altogether different to experience its power where the rubber meets the road of life.

How does the finished work of Christ become *real* to me at my point of need? How does what Christ accomplished for sinners two thousand years ago become vivid and tangible in the moment of temptation, or in the moment when I'm desperately longing for human approval and affection? As I make my way across the wilderness of this life, how does the reality of the ongoing power of the gospel change me, help me, and serve me here and now? How does the gospel connect with my daily grind?

To answer that, it's helpful to remember my purpose and calling in light of the gospel.

OUR PRESENT RESCUE

I'm not sure I can sum up my purpose for living in a sentence, but here's an honest statement I can give you: my passion, as a preacher and a pastor and a Christian, is to show others how the gospel of grace really speaks with practical hope into everything that fallen people will face in this broken world. My goal is to make real for others, at their point of deepest need, the truth of what Jesus did.

The one thing the Bible promises us regarding life in this world is that it will be hard, that we'll face endless trials and temptations and tribulations. Nowhere does the Bible promise that we'll have our best life now—nowhere. In fact, Paul tells young Timothy, "Indeed, all who desire to live a godly life in Christ Jesus will be persecuted" (2 Tim. 3:12).

Many Christians live with what's called an "over-realized

eschatology." Basically what that means is that we're expecting now what God has promised only for later. This causes us to live with unrealistic expectations regarding what we'll face in this world.

Author and counselor Paul Tripp is one of my friends and gospel heroes. Paul says that Christians need a radical reorientation to what he calls the "now-isms" of the gospel. The gospel, in other words, doesn't just rescue us *from* the past and *for* the future; it also rescues us *in the present*—from our fears, from our insecurities, from our lust, from our greed, from our selfishness, from our pride, and more. Most Christian people have a pretty good idea that Jesus has already saved us from sin's penalty, and most of us have a pretty good idea that Jesus will one day save us from sin's presence; but it's the in-between times that we have difficulty understanding—the present power of the gospel.

The gospel is not just a body of content; it's the *power of God* (Rom. 1:16). And it's God's power *in the moment*, at our point of need, whatever that need may be. If we try to live the Christian life on our own, mustering up the willpower to press on, straining forward to impress God with our moral record—we'll only crash and burn.

So how does the gospel apply to us here and now?

EVERYDAY STRUGGLES

As Paul was writing to the Colossians, he understood well that every single day, in a thousand different ways, all of us are offered an endless list of God-replacements. (And in our time, those offers are stoked by the advertising industry spending billions each year enhancing their appeals to give you meaning, purpose, acceptance, approval, significance, and respect.) Like the Colossians (except more so), we're constantly being bombarded with messages to buy these counterfeits. If we don't have a firm grasp of what we already possess, we'll succumb to the pressure.

But in Colossians 2, before Paul points out *what* the Colossians should avoid buying (which he spells out in verses 8–23), he first points out *why* they shouldn't buy it. That's where verses 6 and 7 come in. Let's hear them again: "Therefore, as you received Christ Jesus the Lord, so walk in him, rooted and built up in him and established in the faith, just as you were taught, abounding in thanksgiving."

Paul is reminding them yet again what they already possess, and he wants us to know that the benefits Jesus secured for sinners will always answer our heart's deepest longings; we don't have to look elsewhere, we don't have to look to anything or anyone else besides Jesus to satisfy the deepest cravings and longings of our heart. Only when we come to a better understanding of what we already possess in Jesus will we be able to identify and then resist the counterfeit offerings of this world.

I'm embarrassed to admit it, but on occasion I've spent several minutes trying to find my car keys (only to discover they were in my pocket the whole time), or trying to find my sunglasses (which were on my head the whole time). I was looking for what I already had. And that's what Paul is telling the Colossians to avoid. It was foolish for them to seek out what they already possessed. That was the key issue for them in their daily encounter with life—just as it's the key issue so often with us.

INTERROGATION BY MORNING LIGHT

Thinking out the deep implications of the gospel and applying its powerful reality to all parts of my life is a daily challenge and a daily adventure. Theologically I understand that the gospel didn't just ignite my Christian life but that it's also the fuel that keeps me going and growing every day. My challenge is understanding how this works functionally. So, here are a few questions I go back to all the time that help me make the connection between what Christ accomplished for me and my daily internal grind: Since Jesus secured my pardon and absorbed the Father's wrath on my behalf so that "there is now no condemnation for those who are in Christ Jesus," how does that impact my longing for approval, my tendency to be controlling, and my fear of the unknown? How do the life, death, and resurrection of Christ affect my thirst for security, affection, protection, meaning, and purpose? In other words, how does the finished work of the one "exposed, ravaged, ruined, and resurrected for us" satisfy my deepest daily needs so that I can experience the liberating power of the gospel every day and in every way?

Thinking those things through, asking those questions, is the hard work I believe I'm called to do, the kind of labor Paul speaks of in Philippians 2:12—"work out your own salvation with fear and trembling."

I'm not saying the Christian life is effortless; the real question is *Where are we focusing our efforts?* Are we working hard to perform? Or are we working hard to rest in Christ's performance for us?

THE POWER FOR ABUNDANCE

There's a clear lesson for us about all this on the opening page of Colossians. When Paul prays for the Colossian believers, and then outlines for them what he's praying for them, he's basically giving them a summary of the Christian life, the life of abundance in Christ. Let's return to this passage once more—and as we do, notice Paul's language:

> We have not ceased to pray for you, asking that you may be *filled* with the knowledge of his will in *all* spiritual wisdom and understanding, so as to walk in a manner worthy of the

> Lord, *fully* pleasing to him, bearing fruit in *every* good work and *increasing* in the knowledge of God. May you be strengthened with *all* power, according to his glorious might, for *all* endurance and patience with joy, giving thanks to the Father, who has qualified you to share in the inheritance of the saints in light. (1:9–12)

What Christian wouldn't want a more extensive experience of everything Paul mentions there? But notice where he immediately locates the power for all these things that mark true Christianity:

> He has delivered us from the domain of darkness and *transferred us* to the kingdom of his beloved Son, in whom we have redemption, the forgiveness of sins. (vv. 13–14)

That's the *gospel*. The only way we come to a fuller experience in understanding God's will, and in pleasing God, and in bearing fruit in good works, and in knowing God, and in joyful and patient endurance—the only way those things become an increasing reality for us—is through our fuller understanding and embrace of the gospel, the greater realization that we've already been qualified, delivered, transferred, redeemed, and forgiven.

Paul doesn't pray that the Colossians will find something they don't have; rather he prays they'll grow in their awareness and understanding of what they already have.

RETHINKING PROGRESS

When I came to see that Christian growth doesn't happen by working hard to get something you don't have, but rather it happens by working hard to live in the reality of what you *already* have, this gospel insight radically transformed my life.

The gospel forced me to reconsider the typical way we think

about Christian growth. It forced me to rethink spiritual measurements and maturity; what it means to change, develop, grow; what the pursuit of holiness and the practice of godliness really entails.

For a whole host of reasons, when it comes to measuring spiritual growth and progress, our natural instincts revolve almost exclusively around behavioral improvement. It's understandable.

For example, when we read passages like Colossians 3:5–17, where Paul exhorts the Colossian church to "put on the new self," he uses many behavioral examples: put to death "sexual immorality, impurity, passion, evil desire, and covetousness, which is idolatry." He goes on and exhorts them to put away "anger, wrath, malice, slander," and so on. In verse 12 he switches gears and lists a whole lot of things for us to put on: "kindness, humility, meekness, and patience," just to name a few.

But what's at the *root* of this good and bad fruit? What *produces* both the bad and good behavior Paul addresses here?

Every temptation to sin is, in the moment, a temptation to disbelieve the gospel—the temptation to secure for ourselves in that moment something we think we need in order to be happy, something we don't yet have: meaning, freedom, validation, and so on. Bad behavior happens when we fail to believe that everything we need, in Christ we already have; it happens when we fail to believe in the rich provisional resources that are already ours in the gospel. Conversely, good behavior happens when we daily rest in and receive the finished work of Christ in deeper and deeper ways, smashing any sense of need to secure for ourselves anything beyond what Christ has already secured for us.

Colossians 3:5–17, in other words, provides an illustration of what takes place on the outside when something deeper happens (or doesn't happen) on the inside.

As I've said before, I used to think that when the apostle Paul tells us to work out our salvation, it means go out and get what we don't have—get more patience, get more strength, get more joy, get more love, and so on. But after reading the Bible more carefully, I now understand that Christian growth does not happen by working hard to get something we don't have. Rather, Christian growth happens by working hard to daily swim in the reality of what we do have. Believing again and again the gospel of God's free justifying grace every day—and resting in his verdict—*is* the hard work we're called to.

I think of it this way: the hard work of Christian growth consists primarily in being daily grasped by the fact that God's love for us isn't conditioned by anything we do or don't do. Sanctification is the hard work of giving up our efforts at self-justification. Those efforts are what we're all naturally inclined to do, and it's what makes the sanctification process so grueling and counterintuitive.

In his 2008 movie *The Happening*, writer, producer, and director M. Night Shyamalan unfolds a freaky plot about a mysterious, invisible toxin that causes anyone exposed to it to commit suicide. One of the first signs that the unaware victims have breathed in this self-destructing toxin is that they begin walking backwards, signaling that every natural instinct to go on living and to fight for survival has been reversed. The victim's default survival mechanism is turned upside down.

This, in a sense, is what needs to happen to us when it comes to the way we think about progress in the Christian life. When breathed in, the radical, unconditional, free grace of God reverses every natural instinct regarding what it means to spiritually survive and thrive. Our survival mechanism is to measure spiritual maturity almost exclusively in terms of behavior—what we do and don't do. Only the "toxin" of God's grace can turn that mechanism upside down. Real spiritual progress happens when our typical, natural understanding of progress is rooted out. The key to Christian growth, then, is not first behaving better; it's believing better—believing more deeply what Jesus has already accomplished.

This means that real change happens only as we continuously rediscover the gospel. The progress of the Christian life is "not our movement toward the goal; it's the movement of the goal on us."[1] Sanctification involves God's daily attack on our unbelief—our self-centered refusal to believe that God's approval of us in Christ is full and final. It happens as we daily receive and rest in our unconditional justification. As G. C. Berkouwer said, "The heart of sanctification is the life which feeds on justification."[2]

Second Peter 3:18 succinctly describes growth by saying, "But grow in the grace and knowledge of our Lord and Savior Jesus Christ." Growth always happens "in grace." In other words, the truest measure of our growth is not our behavior (otherwise the Pharisees would have been the godliest people on the planet); it's our grasp of grace—a grasp which involves coming to deeper and deeper terms with the unconditionality of God's love. It's also growth in "the knowledge of our Lord and Savior Jesus Christ." This doesn't simply mean learning facts about Jesus. It means growing in our love for Christ because of what he has already earned and secured for us and then living in a more vital awareness of that grace. Our main problem in the Christian life is not that we don't try hard enough to be good, but that we haven't believed the gospel and received its finished reality into all parts of our life.

Gerhard Forde insightfully (and transparently) calls into question the ways in which we typically think about sanctification and spiritual progress when he writes:

> Am I making progress? If I am really honest, it seems to me that the question is odd, even a little ridiculous. As I get older

and death draws nearer, I don't seem to be getting better. I get a little more impatient, a little more anxious about having perhaps missed what this life has to offer, a little slower, harder to move, a little more sedentary and set in my ways. Am I making progress? Well, maybe it seems as though I sin less, but that may only be because I'm getting tired! It's just too hard to keep indulging the lusts of youth. Is that sanctification? I wouldn't think so! One should not, I expect, mistake encroaching senility for sanctification! But can it be, perhaps, that it is precisely the unconditional gift of grace that helps me to see and admit all that? I hope so. The grace of God should lead us to see the truth about ourselves, and to gain a certain lucidity, a certain humor, a certain down-to-earthness.[3]

Forde rightly shows that when we stop narcissistically focusing on our need to get better, that *is* what it means to get better! When we stop obsessing over our need to improve, that *is* what it means to improve! Remember, the apostle Paul referred to himself as the chief of sinners *at the end of his life*. It was his ability to freely admit that which demonstrated his spiritual maturity—he had nothing to prove or protect because it wasn't about him.

I'm realizing that the sin I need removed daily is precisely my narcissistic understanding of spiritual progress. I think too much about how I'm doing, if I'm growing, whether I'm doing it right or not. I spend too much time pondering my failure, hovering over my spiritual successes, and wondering why, when it's all said and done, I don't seem to be getting that much better. In short, I spend way too much time thinking about me and what I need to do and far too little time thinking about Jesus and what he's already done. And what I've discovered, ironically, is that the more I focus on my need to get better, the worse I actually get. I become neurotic and self-absorbed. Preoccupation with my performance over Christ's performance for me makes me increasingly self-centered and morbidly introspective. Remember, Peter only began to sink when he took his eyes off Jesus and focused on how he was doing. As my friend Rod Rosenbladt said to me recently, "Anytime our natural *incurvitas* (fixture on self) is rattled, shaken, and turned from itself to *that* Man's blood, to *that* Man's cross, then the Devil takes the hindmost!" The more I look into my own heart for peace, the less I find. On the other hand, the more I look to Christ and his promises for peace, the more I find. Christian growth is forgetting about yourself!

So, by all means work! But the hard work is not what you think it is—your personal improvement and moral progress. The hard work is washing your hands of you and resting in Christ's finished work for you, which will inevitably produce personal improvement and moral progress. Progress in obedience happens when our hearts realize that God's love for us does not depend on our progress in obedience. Martin Luther had a point when he said, "It is not imitation that makes sons; it is sonship that makes imitators."

The real question, then, is: What are you going to do now that you don't *have* to do anything? What will your life look like lived under the banner that reads, "It is finished"?

What you'll discover is that once the gospel frees you from having to do *anything* for Jesus, you'll want to do *everything* for Jesus, so that "whether you eat or drink or whatever you do," you'll do it all to the glory of God.

It's this reception of Christ's finished work that helps us experience what Tripp calls the "now-ism's" of the gospel. And that's why I keep telling myself (and others), again and again, *preach the gospel to yourself every single day.*

FULL MATURITY

This hard work we've been speaking of is meant to lead somewhere. There's something that's produced, by God's grace. That something is our maturity, and the Bible speaks of it ultimately as a full and complete maturity.

This full maturity we're called to is something Paul touches on throughout the book of Colossians. Finally, he brings it up again in a very interesting way at the end of this letter. He mentions Epaphras, who was apparently the founder of the church in Colossae, and who was now a prisoner with Paul in Rome. Paul says this about him: "Epaphras, who is one of you, a servant of Christ Jesus, greets you, *always* struggling on your behalf in his prayers, that you may stand *mature* and *fully assured* in *all* the will of God" (4:12). Through the living example of this servant of God, Paul was reminding the Colossian believers again of the fullness of what God in Christ is calling us to experience in the gospel. Through Epaphras's example, he was reminding them once more of what the gospel is meant to lead them to.

The same thought in Paul's heart comes through in his letter to Philemon (written about the same time as his letter to the Colossians). Paul says, "I pray that the sharing of your faith may become effective for the *full knowledge* of every good thing that is in us for the sake of Christ" (Philem. 6). Paul wants his friend to know the comprehensiveness of the *everything* in Christ.

We also see this vision and goal for the fullness of the Christian life in Paul's words to the Romans: "I myself am satisfied about you, my brothers, that you yourselves are *full* of goodness, *filled* with all knowledge and able to instruct one another" (15:14). And also in the words of the apostle James, as he encourages believers to endure their trials: "For you know that the testing of your faith produces steadfastness. And let steadfastness have its *full* effect, that you may be *perfect* and *complete, lacking in nothing*" (James 1:3–4).

HOW CHANGE HAPPENS

All of us, at some level, understand our need to change; and all of us, at some level, even want to change. Because of sin, none of us are fine just the way we are. All of us need to be transformed.

But how does that change happen?

What exactly needs to be changed?

As Christians, what is it that provides us with the resources to fight temptation and to be killing sin in our life? What's the root of all this sin, and where and how can it be dealt with effectively?

Paul helps us answer this in the words of Colossians 3:3–4 (and I hope these words are growing ever more familiar to you): "For you have died, and your life is hidden with Christ in God. When Christ who is your life appears, then you also will appear with him in glory." In these two verses, Paul covers our past, our present, and our future. He says we *have* died; our life *is* hidden with Christ in God (and Christ *is* our life); and we *will* appear with Christ in glory at his return.

God has us fully covered—past, present, future.

In the verses that immediately follow those two, Paul mentions specific sinful behaviors to be done away with in our lives, as he encourages believers to live differently. But throughout Colossians 3, he keeps reminding us of what has already happened to us.

He tells believers, "You too once walked" in these sinful behaviors, "when you were living in them" (v. 7); those things were part of our past. "But *now* you must put them all away . . . seeing that *you have put off* the old self with its practices *and have put on* the new self, which is being renewed in knowledge after the image of its creator " (vv. 8–10).

He's saying, "A radical change has taken place in you—and to succeed in fighting the world, the flesh, and the Devil, you must recognize this change inside you and therefore the resources you already possess."

We're no longer who we used to be. Our old self has died, and we've been raised to a newness of life. God is radically transforming us from the inside out. He's removed our heart of stone and given us a heart of flesh, so that we're now a new creation. The old has passed, and the new has come. As Christians, each of us is fundamentally a changed person.

But if that's true, you may respond, why do I still struggle against the same bad habits? Why do I give in to the same temptations over and over? What's going on?

The Bible makes it clear that if we're a Christian, we're already truly changed—but not yet totally changed. Each of us is a genuinely new creature, but we're not yet a totally new creature. Though we're already fundamentally new, we're not yet completely new. We still struggle with sin because sin has not yet been destroyed in our lives, though it has been dethroned. Sin remains in us, though it no longer reigns in us.

When Jesus returns, we'll finally be totally and absolutely changed. We'll live in God's new world with brand-new bodies and with unbounded energy and passion forever, enjoying what's most enjoyable—God himself—without interruption. But the fullness of that is still in the future.

You are not yet a totally new person. You'll become totally new when Jesus returns and consummates his kingdom on earth as it is in heaven and glorifies all those who are in Christ. The core of your being is no longer sin-centered but God-centered.

But even though the full totality of change is still to come, the change that has *already* taken place is radical and real. Sin used to be the governing authority in us before we knew God; sin was king in our lives, whether or not we've ever realized that or admitted it. But now sin has been overthrown. God is now the governing authority in our lives.

We struggle as we do with sin—the same struggle Paul speaks of in Romans 7—because the sin remaining in us is angry over having been overthrown. It continues its ruthless assaults, employing a guerrilla warfare strategy to continually resist God's new governing authority in and over us.

But amid this raging conflict, Paul wants us to emphatically embrace this fact: *We're no longer sin-centered at our core.* At our core, we're now *God*-centered.

If you're a Christian, then even in the most heated moments of temptation, what you actually desire most deeply is *God*, not sin, because of the transforming work God has done in you. He's changed you at your core. You're a different person now because of the hard surgical work he's done inside you.

That's why such an important part of fending off temptation—whether it be something Paul lists in verses 5 and 8 of Colossians 3 ("sexual immorality, impurity, passion, evil desire, and covetousness, which is idolatry," or "anger, wrath, malice, slander, and obscene talk"), or something else—what's important is simply to first come to terms with *who you are*, what you've been remade to be. Bring that reality into the moment of temptation, and be reminded by the gospel of who you are now, and of what you want most, even in the face of sin's deception about what you really desire. Identity (who we are) precedes practicality (what we do).

If we would just stop and remember the gospel, we would realize that God really is what we want most, even in our worst moments, no matter how strong the temptation we're battling.

Lasting behavioral change happens as you grow in your understanding of the gospel, and then as you learn to receive and rest in—at your point of deepest need—everything Jesus secured for you.

WHAT ABOUT ACCOUNTABILITY IN THE PROCESS OF CHANGE?

At different times in my life I've been a part of what's called an "accountability group." You know the ones I'm talking about—where you and a small group of "friends" arrange for a time each week to get together and pick each other apart, uncovering layer after layer after layer of sin. All parties involved believe that the guiltier we feel, the more holy we are. You confess your sin to your friends, but it's never enough; no matter what you unveil, they're always looking for you to uncover something deeper, darker, and more embarrassing than what you've fessed up to. It's usually done with such persistent invasion that you get the feeling they're desperately looking for something in you that will make them feel better about themselves. Well, I hate those groups!

The reason I hate the kind of group described above is that their focus is primarily (almost exclusively, in my experience) on our sin, and not on our Savior. Because of this, these groups breed self-righteousness, guilt, and the almost irresistible temptation to pretend—to be less than honest. I can't tell you how many times I've been in accountability groups where there has been little to no attention given to the gospel whatsoever. There's no reminder of what Christ has done for our sin—cleansing us from its guilt *and* power—and the resources that are already ours by virtue of our union with him. These groups produce a "do more, try harder" moralism that robs us of the joy and freedom Jesus paid dearly to secure for us. They start with the narcissistic presupposition that Christianity is all about cleaning up and getting better—it's all about personal improvement. *But that's not Christianity!*

When *the* goal becomes conquering our sin instead of soaking in the conquest of our Savior, instead of growing stronger and more mature, we actually begin to shrink spiritually. Sinclair Ferguson rightly points this out:

> Those who have almost forgotten about their own spirituality because their focus is so exclusively on their union with Jesus Christ and what He has accomplished are those who are

growing and exhibiting fruitfulness. Historically speaking, whenever the piety of a particular group is focused on our spirituality, that piety will eventually exhaust itself on its own resources. Only when our piety forgets about us and focuses on Jesus Christ will our piety be nourished by the ongoing resources the Spirit brings to us from the source of all true piety, our Lord Jesus Christ.[4]

Like I said above, when we (or our friends) focus mostly on our need to get better, we actually get worse. We become neurotic and self-absorbed. Preoccupation with our guilt (instead of with God's grace) makes us increasingly myopic and self-interested. Real Christian growth, according to the seventeenth-century Puritan Jeremiah Burroughs, "comes not so much from our struggling and endeavors and resolutions, as it comes flowing to us from our union with him."

To be sure, we're called to "mortify the flesh," "put to death the misdeeds of the body," "cut off our hand," and "gouge out our eye" if they cause us to sin—and we need the help of other people to get this done. Sanctification is a community project.

But the sin that gives rise to our sinful behavior is a preoccupation with ourselves. That's the root sin that needs to be mortified. That's the under-the-surface sin that gives birth to our misdeeds. The first sin that needs to be rooted out and attacked is not immoral behavior; it's immoral belief—the belief that my Christian life is all about my moral and spiritual progress.

Again (I can't stress this enough), it's so important to understand that Christianity is not first about our getting better, our obedience, our behavior, and our daily victory over remaining sin—as important as all these are. It's first about Jesus! It's about his person and substitutionary work—his incarnation, life, death, resurrection, ascension, session, and promised return. We're justified—and sanctified—by grace alone through faith alone in the finished work of Christ alone.

Therefore, the accountability I need is the kind that corrects my natural tendency to focus on me—*my* obedience (or lack thereof), *my* performance (good or bad), *my* holiness—instead of on Christ and *his* obedience, *his* performance, and *his* holiness for me. We all possess a natural proclivity to turn God's good news announcement that we've been set free into a narcissistic program of self-improvement. We need to be held accountable for that!

So, instead of trying to fix one another, why don't we "stir one another up to love and good deeds" by daily reminding one another, in humble love, of the riches we already possess in Christ? All the "good stuff" that's ours already in Christ settles at the bottom when we focus on ourselves more than on Jesus (after all, on the waters of the Sea of Galilee Peter began to sink only when he took his eyes off Jesus and focused on his performance).

Our greatest need is to look at Christ more than we look at ourselves, because the gospel is not our work for Jesus, but Jesus's work for us. As Sinclair Ferguson has said, "The evangelical orientation is inward and subjective. We are far better at looking inward than we are at looking outward. Instead, we need to expend our energies admiring, exploring, expositing, and extolling Jesus Christ."[5] It takes the loving act of our Christian brothers and sisters to remind us every day of the gospel—that everything we need, and everything we look for in things smaller than Jesus, is already ours "in Christ." When we do this, the "good stuff" rises to the top.

Let me remind you again of the old Puritan statement that far too many Christians live beneath the level of their privileges. I need to be told by those around me that every time I sin, I'm momentarily suffering from an identity crisis: forgetting who I *actually* belong to, what I *really* want at my remade core, and all that is *already* mine in Christ. I need my real friends to remind me of this—every day. *Please tell me again and again that God doesn't love me more when I obey or less when I disobey.* Knowing this actually enlarges my heart for God and therefore shrinks my hunger for sin. *So don't let me forget it.* My life depends on it!

I'm all for accountability, but I'm for a certain kind of it—the kind that forces us to reckon with the scandalous nature of God's unconditional love for us because of Christ's finished work on our behalf. I believe in the need to repent and to confess our sins to one another (James 5:16). But only by reckoning with God's unconditional love in the face of our ongoing failure can we move toward genuine, heart-felt confession of sin and repentance. God's kindness, after all, "is meant to lead you to repentance" (Rom. 2:4).

In an excellent article entitled "Does Justification Still Matter?" Mike Horton raises the same concern I do with regard to our natural tendency to focus inward more than Christ-ward. He writes:

> Most people in the pew . . . are simply not acquainted with the doctrine of justification. Often, it is not a part of the diet of preaching and church life, much less a dominant theme in the Christian subculture. With either stern rigor or happy tips for better living, "fundamentalists" and "progressives" alike smother the gospel in moralism, through constant exhortations to personal transformation that keep the sheep looking to themselves rather than looking outside of themselves to Christ. . . . The average feature article in [Christian magazines] or Christian best-sellers is concerned with "good works"-trends in spirituality, social activism, church growth, and discipleship. However, it's pretty clear that justification is simply not on the radar. Even where it is not outright rejected, it is often ignored. Perhaps the forgiveness of sins and justification are appropriate for "getting saved," but then comes the real business of Christian living—as if there could be any genuine holiness of life that did not arise out of a perpetual confidence that "there is therefore now no condemnation to those who are in Christ Jesus" (Romans 8:1).[6]

Because we're so naturally prone to look at ourselves and our performance more than we look to Christ and his performance, we need constant reminders of the gospel. As Horton says, there can be no genuine holiness of life that does not arise out of a perpetual confidence that "there is therefore now no condemnation to those who are in Christ Jesus" (Rom. 8:1). The only way to deal with remaining sin long-term is to develop a distaste for it in light of the glorious acceptance, security, and forgiveness we already possess in Christ. I need to be reminded of this all the time, every day. Because the fact is, guilt doesn't produce holiness; grace does.

What Paul did for the Colossians (repeatedly reminding them of the treasure they already had in Christ) is what we all need our Christian brothers and sisters to do for us as well: remind us first of what's been done, not what we must do.

The bottom line is this, Christian: because of Christ's work on your behalf, God doesn't dwell on your sin the way you do. So, relax, and rejoice, and you'll actually start to get better. The irony, of course, is that it's only when we stop obsessing over our own need to be holy and focus instead on the beauty of Christ's holiness that we actually become more holy! Not to mention that we also start to become a lot easier to live with.

SOMETHING BETTER THAN IMITATING CHRIST

Michael Horton in *The Gospel-Driven Life* emphasizes that what we're called to do in our Christian lives is not merely to imitate Christ, though it does involve a conformity to Christ. He reminds us that Paul's teaching about Christ gives us "something far greater than an example to imitate":

He calls us not simply to imitate Christ but to be crucified, buried, and raised with him. Since we *are* in Christ, we must act accordingly: daily putting to death the deeds of unrighteousness, and bearing the fruit of our union with him—but union with Christ. But before he speaks an imperative, he announces the indicative of the gospel: Christ's saving work has accomplished far more than we imagined. The Spirit's work of uniting us to Christ makes us not mere imitators but living members of his body. We are incorporated—baptized—into Christ's death, burial and resurrection. Paul does not say, "Be like Jesus." He says, "You *are* like Jesus. He is the head, and you are part of his body; he is the first fruits and you are the rest of the harvest. As goes the head, so go the members. You are now swept by your forerunner into the new creation. So how can you continue living as if none of this ever happened?"[7]

Elyse Fitzpatrick summarizes it in this simple phrase: "Be who you are."[8]

SECRET OF MATURITY

The gospel's secret of maturity is this: we become more spiritually mature when we focus less on what we need to do for God and focus more on all that God has already done for us.

That's the irony of the gospel, and we find it throughout the Bible. It's unavoidable, inescapable.

We actually perform better in life as we grow in understanding that our relationship with God is based on Christ's performance for us, not on our performance for him. We mature more when we focus less on our performance for Jesus and more on Jesus's performance for us, as we sing:

Nothing in my hand I bring,
simply to thy cross I cling.

It's Jesus plus nothing equals everything.

DON'T FORGET

At the beginning of Peter's second epistle, where he tells us that God has given us his very great and precious promises, and that God's power has granted us "all things that pertain to life and godliness," Peter also tells us that this allows us to "become partakers of the divine nature, having escaped from the corruption that is in the world because of sinful desire" (1:4).

He then proceeds to cast a vision of our continued growth and development in Christian maturity. He exhorts believers to grow spiritually and to work out in their lives what God has worked in. He writes, "For this very reason, make every effort to supplement your faith with virtue, and virtue with knowledge, and knowledge with self-control, and self-control with steadfastness, and steadfastness with godliness, and godliness with brotherly affection, and brotherly affection with love" (vv. 5–7).

His next statement reminds us again of the abundance God has designed for the Christian life: "For if these qualities are yours and are increasing, they keep you from being ineffective or unfruitful in the knowledge of our Lord Jesus Christ" (v. 8).

Then he shows us again why it's so important to build everything in our lives on the gospel. He says, "For whoever lacks these qualities is so nearsighted that he is blind, *having forgotten that he was cleansed from his former sins*" (v. 9).

Gospel-driven change is rooted in remembrance. The way God grows us, develops us, and matures us is by reminding us of what he has already done for us in Christ.

It's as you grow in your awareness of what Christ has already accomplished for you that you begin to increasingly take on the Christian qualities and virtues that Peter outlines in 2 Peter 1.

THE LAW AND THE GOSPEL

With all the words I've written against legalism in this book, you may be wondering: "What place should God's law have in the life of a Christian, especially as we press forward toward greater maturity?" You may be thinking, "I clearly understand that keeping the rules and cleaning myself up is definitely not the message of Christianity. I realize that our right standing with God is dependent on Christ's obedience for us and not on our obedience and ability to keep the law. I get that. But what role should God's commands play in my life, if any?"

Very important question! Paul says in Romans 7:12, "The law is holy, and the commandment is holy and righteous and good." He's thinking particularly there about God's moral commands that are still binding on us today (rather than about sacrificial and ceremonial laws in the Old Testament that already have been entirely fulfilled in Christ). This moral law is what we find summarized in the Ten Commandments and summarized even further by Jesus when he said this: "You shall love the Lord your God with all your heart and with all your soul and with all your mind. This is the great and first commandment. And a second is like it: You shall love your neighbor as yourself. On these two commandments depend all the Law and the Prophets" (Matt. 22:37–40).

The moral law of God is entirely good. All the imperatives in the Bible, everything God asks us to do, are good because God is good. His commands and directives and precepts are an accurate reflection of the character of God.

This very aspect of the law—its goodness, reflecting God's goodness—is the reason that God's law causes Paul to see his own sin, as he explains in Romans 7:7–14. The law is like a mirror, showing all of us who we really are, as well as what we really need.

The problem is not God's law; the problem, as Paul makes

clear in Romans 7, is us. This is the inward struggle Paul speaks of in Romans 7 (and which rages inside all believers). It's a hard, painful battle between God's standards and our sin. Paul unfolds his own struggle with powerful detail in this chapter. Finally he cries out, "Wretched man that I am! Who will deliver me from this body of death?" (v. 24). He knows he's hopeless and helpless whenever he stares at the law of God.

But his rescue comes as he turns his gaze to Jesus, which Paul does in the very next verse: "Thanks be to God through Jesus Christ our Lord!" (v. 25). Paul, as a believer in Christ, has allowed the law to continue driving him to the gospel. And that's what we're to do as well.

WANTING WHAT GOD WANTS

Finally, one of the indicators that we're firmly on the path of Christian growth—one of the marks of a truly maturing Christian—is that we begin to love the things God loves, and to want the things God wants, and to hate the things God hates. In this regard, the law guides us as well, and it guides wisely. It tells us what God wants and who God is. Yes, the law is good.

But while the law guides, it does not give. It has the power to reveal sin but not the power to remove sin. It simply cannot engender what it commands. The law shows us what godliness is, but it cannot make us godly like the gospel can. The law shows us what a sanctified life looks like, but it does not have sanctifying power as the gospel does. So, apart from the gospel, the law crushes. The law shows us what to do. The gospel announces what God has done. The law directs us, but only the gospel can drive us. It's very important to keep these distinctions in mind.

Let me stress again that this is not a matter of whether obedience to God's law is important, either to us or to God. Of course it's important. The question is: *Where does our power to obey God's commands come from?* Does it come from the gospel—from what God has done for us? Or does it come from the law—from what we must do? That contrast is another way of asking, Does the power come from *God* or from *you?* It's that simple.

Paul lays out the intensity of his struggle in Romans 7 to make it clear that although the law can no longer condemn us (because Jesus has kept it perfectly on our behalf), it's still unable to produce in us the desire to keep it. It can only tell us what God requires, which it does. But the law is not the gospel.

Paul's conclusion in Romans 7— "Thanks be to God through Jesus Christ our Lord"—demonstrates gratitude for the fact that Jesus has come to do for us what we could never do for ourselves. Jesus has perfectly fulfilled the law of God on our behalf so that now our standing with God, our relationship with God, is based first not on our obedience but on Christ's obedience. Paul finds hope in Jesus—and so must we.

From that expression of gratitude to Jesus, Paul then goes forward into the exhilarating words we find throughout chapter 8 in Romans, beginning with this liberating statement: "There is therefore now no condemnation for those who are in Christ Jesus. For the law of the Spirit of life has *set you free in Christ Jesus* from the law of sin and death" (vv. 1–2).

The gospel of Christ gives us the freedom that the law never could.

To some, this will sound like a cop-out that's antinomian ("anti-law"—a lawless, obligation-free version of Christianity). After all, doesn't the American church need to be shaken out of its comfort zone? Yes, but you don't do it by giving them law; you do it by giving them gospel.

Writing in response to a recent *Christianity Today* article in which the writer voices concern about the lack of emphasis on personal holiness and radical obedience in this generation of

Christians, my friend Dane Ortlund shows how there are two ways to address this:

> One way is to balance gospel grace with exhortations to holiness, as if both need equal air time lest we fall into legalism on one side (neglecting grace) or antinomianism on the other (neglecting holiness). The other way, which I believe is the right and biblical way, is to so startle this restraint-free culture with the gospel of free justification that the functional justifications of human approval, moral performance, sexual indulgence, or big bank accounts begin to lose their vice-like grip on human hearts, and their emptiness is exposed in all its fraudulence. It sounds backward, but the path to holiness is through (not beyond) the grace of the gospel, because only undeserved grace can truly melt and transform the heart. The solution to restraint-free immorality is not morality. The solution to immorality is the free grace of God—grace so free that it will be (mis)heard by some as a license to sin with impunity. The route by which the New Testament exhorts radical obedience is not by tempering grace but by driving it home all the more deeply. Let's pursue holiness. And let's pursue it centrally through enjoying the gospel, the same gospel that got us in and the same gospel that liberates us afresh each day (1 Cor. 15:1–2; Gal. 2:14; Col. 1:23; 2:6). As G. C. Berkouwer wisely remarked, "The heart of sanctification is the life which feeds on justification."[9]

As I mentioned earlier, one of my responsibilities as a pastor is to disciple people into a deeper understanding of obedience—teaching them to say no to the things God hates and yes to the things God loves. But all too often I've wrongly concluded that the only way to keep licentious people in line is to give them more rules—to lay down the law. In my desire as both a pastor and a parent to see those under my care become more radical in their obedience to God, I have often fallen into the trap of going from the law (cutting off hope) to the gospel (forgiveness and life) and then back to the law, as if the gospel handled justification but can't keep up with sanctification. The fact is, however, that the only way licentious people start to obey is when they get a taste of God's radical, unconditional acceptance of sinners. In Romans 6:1–4, Paul answers antinomianism (lawlessness) not with more law but with more gospel! Paul could have easily put the brakes on grace and given the law in this passage, but instead he gives more grace—grace upon grace. In other words, licentious people aren't those who believe the gospel of God's free grace too much, but too little. The irony of gospel-based sanctification is that those who end up obeying more are those who increasingly realize that their standing with God is *not* based on their obedience but on Christ's. As John Bunyan memorably put it:

> "Run, John, run," the law demands,
> but gives me neither feet nor hands.
> Better news the Gospel brings,
> It bids me fly and gives me wings.

To say, however, that the law has no power to change us *in no way* reduces its ongoing role in the life of the Christian. We just have to understand the precise role it plays for us today. The law now serves us by showing us how to love God and others, and it makes us thankful for Jesus when we break it. Only the gospel, however, empowers us to keep the law. And when we fail to keep it, the gospel brings comfort by reminding us that God's infinite approval doesn't depend on our keeping of the law but on Christ's keeping of the law on our behalf.

And guess what? This makes me want to obey him more, not less! As Spurgeon wrote, "When I thought God was hard, I found it easy to sin; but when I found God so kind, so good, so overflowing with compassion, I smote upon my breast to think that I could ever have rebelled against One who loved me so, and sought my good."[10]

Therefore, it's the gospel (what Jesus has done) that alone can give God-honoring animation to our obedience. The power to obey comes from being moved and motivated by the completed work of Jesus for us. The fuel to do good flows from what's already been done. So again, while the law directs us, only the gospel can drive us.

A friend of mine recently put it to me this way: the law is like a set of railroad tracks. The tracks provide no power for the train but the train must stay on the tracks in order to function. The law never gives any power to do what it commands. Only the gospel has power, as it were, to move the train.

Recognizing the continual need of the gospel for Christian people as much as the initial need of the gospel for non-Christian people, J. Gresham Machen wrote, "What I need first of all is not exhortation, but a gospel; not directions for saving myself but knowledge of how God has saved me."

The gospel of amazing grace gets us in, keeps us in, and will eventually get us to the finish line. It's all of grace!

12

ALL GLORIOUS

Together in these pages, you and I have been given a small glimpse of the *everything* that's ours in Christ, and what all this can mean for us this very day and hour.

Let's celebrate it now—in the small way, at least, that reading and reflecting on this chapter represents. But we also know that very soon, we'll all celebrate in a huge way, fully and forever.

Already we can celebrate freely because we've come to see, more clearly than ever, that our identity and purpose and significance aren't located in anything we can do or attain. No, it's all in Christ. We've heard Paul's words in Colossians 3:4 ringing out: "When Christ who is your life . . . " He didn't say, "Christ who's *a part of* your life," but "Christ, who *is* your life."

Jesus *is* our life.

"What is your life?" James asks us (James 4:14).

"Jesus," we can faithfully and truthfully answer.

He's your life now, he's my life now, and in eternity he will be for us an even fuller and freer life than we can ever imagine. For we remember the assurance of his word through his servant Paul: "Your *life* is hidden with Christ in God" (Col. 3:3).

"I DEFY YOU"

The power of that last verse is on good display in this famous story of the fourth-century church father Chrysostom (as summarized here by Ray Ortlund):

When John Chrysostom was brought before the empress Eudoxia, she threatened him with banishment if he insisted on his Christian independence as a preacher.

"You cannot banish me, for this world is my Father's house."

"But I will kill you," said the empress.

"No, you cannot, for my life is hid with Christ in God," said John.

"I will take away your treasures."

"No, you cannot, for my treasure is in heaven and my heart is there."

"But I will drive you away from your friends and you will have no one left."

"No, you cannot, for I have a Friend in heaven from whom you cannot separate me. I defy you, for there is nothing you can do to harm me."[1]

That's a story that I shared in our church on a Sunday morning in September of 2009. It was the morning when, as a result of the petition drive to force my ouster from our church's pastorate, another congregational vote regarding me was being taken after the service. I was there to preach before that vote took place; to say the least, it was an awkward environment for a preacher to experience. Pockets of people were there to take me down. As I preached, they stared at me with looks that could kill.

I preached my guts out—it was the freest I've ever been in the pulpit. I was realizing *in the moment* that Jesus plus nothing equals everything. I was colorfully alive to the reality that no one in the room that morning could take away anything I'd received from Jesus, which was everything. I was free! Completely free! I closed my sermon that morning by saying:

To all who are willing to change and serve and grow and be stretched and lose it all for the sake of Christ, God bless you. To those who, like Jesus, are ready to take up their cross and "go outside the camp"—who understand it's better to give than to receive, to be self-sacrificial rather than self-serving, to look out

for the interests of others before your own interests—I thank
you. To those who are willing to be defined by—and to fight for—
the treasures of Christ, not the traditions of men—we need you!

God cannot be stopped; regardless of what happens, he
will have his way and win the day. God is moving me forward
one way or another, and I will consider it a high and holy privilege to serve and love and teach and lay my life down for those
who move ahead with us. We will move ahead together—side
by side, back to back—in order to spread God's renown in this
city, in our time. To live is Christ, to die is gain!

Bracing my mind and heart that morning was the example of
Chrysostom's boldness. And encouraging me even more was the
bold confidence that rightfully belongs to all of us as believers, as
I'd been freshly enjoying through Paul's teaching in Colossians.

I didn't stay for the meeting afterward because my father was
dying in the hospital after a liver transplant, and I went to see
him. That fact, on top of the situation at church, made that day
the most difficult Sunday of my life.

As it turned out, the congregational vote that day was over-
whelmingly in favor of keeping me as the church's pastor.

And since that time—two years ago—I'm pleased to say that
God has seen fit to launch a gospel "riot" at Coral Ridge. The *everything* of God's gospel is setting people free, creating great joy, and
reaching our needy city.

But what was far more important that day than any "victory at
the polls" was the ever-freeing, presently empowering dynamics
of the gospel I was rediscovering through the book of Colossians.
I was rediscovering the joy and celebration and hope that accom-
panies gospel freedom.

BROUGHT TO COMPLETION

You and I can celebrate because the day is coming when everything God has been working into our lives—through all those

days and months and years of challenges and adversities, and all those obstacles and ordeals, all those tasks and opportunities, all those heartaches and losses—will all finally be brought to completion, and the finished product will be on display.

"I am sure of this," Paul says, and so are we: "that he who began a good work in you will bring it to *completion* at the day of Jesus Christ" (Phil. 1:6).

Paul, the man who always prayed for all believers everywhere, and told us to do the same (Eph. 6:18; Col. 2:1), will be with us to see the complete answers to all those prayers, like these:

> Now may the God of peace himself sanctify you *completely*, and may your whole spirit and soul and body be kept blameless at the coming of our Lord Jesus Christ. He who calls you is faithful; he will surely do it. (1 Thess. 5:23–24)

> We *always* pray for you, that our God may make you worthy of his calling and may fulfill *every* resolve for good and every work of faith by his power. (2 Thess. 1:11)

When the day of completion and resolution comes for all that God is doing in and through us, we won't hesitate to celebrate. And we'll get ready for it *now*, learning to deeply understand his gospel more and more, and all that it's accomplishing in our lives; and we say with David, "I meditate on *all* that you have done; I ponder the work of your hands" (Ps. 143:5).

Even now we sing in celebration with the Psalms, "The word of the LORD is upright, and all his work is done in faithfulness" (33:4); "Full of splendor and majesty is his work, and his righteousness endures forever" (111:3).

ALL THINGS NEW

We'll celebrate as we open wide our eyes and minds and hearts to see the cosmic scope of all that God is doing now, and will do.

We'll celebrate all the everlasting newness he has promised, for we hear his wider word for us in Isaiah's prophecy: "From this time forth I announce to you new things, hidden things that you have not known" (Isa. 48:6).

And even more, loud and clear, we hear the voice from his eternal throne: "Behold, I am making all things new" (Rev. 21:5). And we'll see it actually happen.

The cosmic groans will finally stop, the groans of "the whole creation" that Paul mentions in Romans 8:22. Jesus, when he returns, will complete the process of renewing all things. The "peace on earth" that was announced by the angel on the night he was born will become a universal, permanent actuality. Everything crooked will be made straight, everything rough will be made smooth, everything wrong will be righted; every injustice will be permanently corrected. The fraying fabric of our fallen world and the fraying fabric of our lives will be fully and perfectly rewoven. Everything connected to Jesus will live in perfect harmony and shalom will rule. Everything will be the way it was originally intended to be.

And that means, for those who've found forgiveness of sins through the gospel of Christ, that suddenly there'll be no more sickness, no more dying, no more tears, no more division, no more tension. Those who trust in Jesus will enjoy new, sinless bodies in a brand-new sinless world. All that causes us pain and discomfort will be destroyed. We'll live forever in unimaginable fulfillment.

The best is yet to come, because God worked in the gospel of Christ "to reconcile to himself all things, whether on earth or in heaven, making peace by the blood of his cross" (Col. 1:20).

We'll see a new city "coming down out of heaven from God" (Rev. 21:2), to regenerate and resurrect our broken world. Jesus is coming to resurrect the entire cosmic order—that's how big his salvation is. And it calls for our biggest celebration.

REIGNING WITH CHRIST

So we'll celebrate, knowing that the *everything* our Lord gives us in the gospel includes our reigning with him.

It will be just as Jesus told us: "Fear not, little flock," he said, "for it is your Father's good pleasure to give you the kingdom" (Luke 12:32).

And in the glorified revelation of himself to John and to the churches, our Savior made this promise: "The one who conquers, I will grant him to sit with me on my throne, as I also conquered and sat down with my Father on his throne" (Rev. 3:21).

We celebrate, knowing that because of the gospel, the goodness and grace of God will bring us eternal reward from God. We'll see the actual fulfillment of Jesus's words from the mountainside: "Rejoice and be glad, for your reward is great in heaven" (Matt. 5:12).

EVERLASTING

We'll celebrate, knowing that our *everything* in Christ is so much, so huge, it will take us all of eternity to receive it and to embrace it.

We'll be forever in him, forever close, all according to his certain promise: "and so we will *always* be with the Lord" (1 Thess. 4:17).

The fullness of time will bring the fullness of blessing; the eternal that we've *already* been granted title to—God "loved us and gave us *eternal* comfort," Paul says (2 Thess. 2:16)—will become ours in actual experience.

We'll celebrate forever because the encouragement and the comfort and the glory will last forever; our fullness of blessing, our *everything*, will be "an eternal weight of glory beyond all comparison" (2 Cor. 4:17).

SPECIFICS

But a pause here, a check. *Everything.* Sometimes the word doesn't really register. It can seem so general and vague—*everything*?

Especially when we're thinking about our distant eternal future, in a reborn age and environment that we've heard about, yet never actually known, so far.

But Jesus helps us here. In God's promise to "the one who conquers"—the one who, by faith, we are united to—we are graced with beautiful, intriguing specifics that tantalize all our senses, giving us rich fare for reflection and reassurance in our troubled moments now:

> To the one who conquers I will grant to eat of the tree of life, which is in the paradise of God. (Rev. 2:7)

> The one who conquers will not be hurt by the second death. (Rev. 2:11)

> To the one who conquers I will give some of the hidden manna, and I will give him a white stone, with a new name written on the stone that no one knows except the one who receives it. (Rev. 2:17)

> The one who conquers and who keeps my works until the end, to him I will give authority over the nations, and he will rule them with a rod of iron, as when earthen pots are broken in pieces, even as I myself have received authority from my Father. And I will give him the morning star. (Rev. 2:26–28)

> The one who conquers will be clothed thus in white garments, and I will never blot his name out of the book of life. I will confess his name before my Father and before his angels. (Rev. 3:5)

> The one who conquers, I will make him a pillar in the temple of my God. Never shall he go out of it, and I will write on him the name of my God, and the name of the city of my God, the new Jerusalem, which comes down from my God out of heaven, and my own new name. (Rev. 3:12)

I counsel you to buy from me gold refined by fire, so that you may be rich, and white garments so that you may clothe yourself and the shame of your nakedness may not be seen, and salve to anoint your eyes, so that you may see. (Rev. 3:18)

The one who conquers, I will grant him to sit with me on my throne, as I also conquered and sat down with my Father on his throne. (Rev. 3:21)

WORTHY OF OUR EVERYTHING

So we celebrate. We celebrate with worship, because the Lord's everything is worthy of our everything.

We celebrate because he's put us on the path of fulfillment for our deepest longing, the same profoundest yearning that David had: "One thing have I asked of the LORD, that will I seek after: that I may dwell in the house of the LORD all the days of my life, to gaze upon the beauty of the LORD and to inquire in his temple" (Ps. 27:4). This was not the "one thing" we once sought for, but now, by the grace of the gospel of Christ, it genuinely is.

Because of the gospel, we've come to see that he alone is worthy to receive our everything. Consider the worship words we find in Revelation: "Worthy are you, our Lord and God, to receive *glory and honor and power*" (Rev. 4:11).

Jesus became nothing so that we might have everything. So we'll join the angelic throng in his praise, "saying with a loud voice, 'Worthy is the Lamb who was slain, to receive power and wealth and wisdom and might and honor and glory and blessing!'" (Rev. 5:12).

The day is coming soon when we'll join forever that eternal sacrifice of praise, but even now we celebrate. Even now we say with David, "I will give thanks to the LORD with *my whole heart*; I will recount *all* of your wonderful deeds" (Ps. 9:1).

ALL THE WORLD'S WORSHIP

We celebrate as we join in the worship that catches up and captures everything around us.

God's worship commands *will* be fully obeyed: "Let everything that has breath praise the LORD! Praise the LORD!" (Ps. 150:6); "Let all the earth fear the LORD; let all the inhabitants of the world stand in awe of him!" (Ps. 33:8); "Let heaven and earth praise him, the seas and everything that moves in them" (Ps. 69:34).

We'll join the angels as they obey their charge to glorify Jesus: "Let all God's angels worship him" (Heb. 1:6)

The cosmic worship that Jesus could foresee from the cross—as foretold in the messianic words of Psalm 22, words that Jesus pointed to in his suffering—will find its fulfillment:

> All the ends of the earth shall remember
> > and turn to the LORD,
> and all the families of the nations
> > shall worship before you. . . .
> All the prosperous of the earth eat and worship;
> > before him shall bow all who go down to the dust,
> > even the one who could not keep himself alive.
> Posterity shall serve him;
> > it shall be told of the Lord to the coming generation;
> they shall come and proclaim his righteousness to a people
> yet unborn,
> > that he has done it. (Ps. 22:27–31)

It's the world's worship destiny that Paul teaches us about:

> Therefore God has highly exalted him and bestowed on him the name that is above *every* name, so that at the name of Jesus *every* knee should bow, in heaven and on earth and under the earth, and *every* tongue confess that Jesus Christ is Lord, to the glory of God the Father. (Phil. 2:9–11)

We'll join our own voices in the worship gathering that Paul could foresee in the day of Christ's return, "when he comes on that day to be glorified in his saints, and to be marveled at among all who have believed" (2 Thess. 1:10).

OUR FILLED-UP EARTH

We celebrate because of something sweeping over this world. Already the entire earth is touched by God's fullness, but someday soon it will become greater still.

Already the seraphim call to each other and say, "Holy, holy, holy is the LORD of hosts; *the whole earth is full of his glory!*" (Isa. 6:3).

Already David tells forth God's praise: "He loves righteousness and justice; the earth is *full* of the steadfast love of the LORD" (Ps. 33:5). Yes, already the psalmist declares to him, "The earth, O LORD, is *full* of your steadfast love" (Ps. 119:64).

But a still greater saturation is coming, like a global tsunami that swells and never retreats: "For the earth will be filled with the knowledge of the glory of the LORD as the waters cover the sea" (Hab. 2:14). The *everything* of the Lord, the fullness he currently shares with us but that we will experience perfectly one day, is a tidal wave of glory.

HOW GREAT THE GLORY

We celebrate, because of the glory we will see and share. We've taken to heart God's promise to us through Paul's words to the Colossians: "When Christ who is your life appears, then you also will appear with him in glory" (3:4).

We'll gaze on the temple of the Lord—the real one, and no shadow—and we'll know this reality: "In his temple all cry, 'Glory!'" (Ps. 29:9).

We'll flex our spiritual muscles under the "eternal weight of glory beyond all comparison" (2 Cor. 4:17), as we make much of the Lord's greatness—engaging with it, loving it, exulting in it, seeing it more and more.

You'll call to me, and I'll call to you, and we'll say, "Oh, magnify the LORD with me, and let us exalt his name together!" (Ps. 34:3). We'll forever join our voices with Mary's: "My soul magnifies the Lord, and my spirit rejoices in God my Savior" (Luke 1:46–47).

We'll finally and fully understand what Paul was saying about Jesus in 2 Corinthians 1:20: "For all the promises of God find their Yes in him. That is why it is through him that we utter our Amen to God for his glory."

We'll celebrate that glory even now, for you and I have been enabled to say with Paul, "I consider that the sufferings of this present time are not worth comparing with the glory that is to be revealed to us" (Rom. 8:18).

ALWAYS REJOICING

In this life and in this world, as we "walk in him" (Col. 2:6) in the light of the gospel of Christ, we share Paul's circumstances and his experience of the everything: "as sorrowful, yet always rejoicing; as poor, yet making many rich; as having nothing, yet possessing everything" (2 Cor. 6:10). In our present circumstances, the sorrow can be piercingly real and our sense of lack potently felt (inwardly especially).

But we hear our Savior's promises. We hear him say, "You have sorrow now, but I will see you . . . and your hearts will rejoice, and no one will take your joy from you" (John 16:22). Our joy will cling to us forever.

So we celebrate, because we know that whatever taste of sorrow and longing and incompleteness we experience now will soon be all forgotten. Jesus, our source of everything, comforts and cheers us with these words: "Blessed are you who are hungry now, for you shall be *satisfied*. Blessed are you who weep now, for you shall *laugh*" (Luke 6:21). His *everything* will finally and completely fill us—and so will his laughter!

Knowing that the laughter's coming—exuberant, hilarious, uproarious—and coming soon, we can endure anything now. We aren't unaware of the grief and the pain. And when it grows worse in the hours and days we have remaining in this life, it won't catch us offguard, because he's already told us, in all seriousness, yet calmly and lovingly: "Beloved, do not be surprised at the fiery trial when it comes upon you to test you, as though something strange were happening to you. But rejoice insofar as you share Christ's sufferings, that you may also rejoice and be glad when his glory is revealed" (1 Pet. 4:12–13).

The day's coming soon when we'll fully grasp his everything and more, all that's been promised us in his glorious gospel of Christ. On that day, everything within you and me will be unleashed to rejoice in him forever. So celebrate *now*, today, this very hour, resting gladly in him.

IT IS FINISHED

To close this book, let me retell a story that my friend Steve Brown tells that illustrates well how God deals with us according to the finished work of Christ.

He says that one time his daughter Robin found herself in a very difficult English literature course that she desperately wanted to get out of. She sat there on her first day and thought, "If I don't transfer out of this class, I'm going to fail. The other people in this class are much smarter than me. I can't do this." She came home with tears in her eyes and begged her dad to help her get out of the class so she could take a regular English course. Steve said, "Of course." So the next day he took her down to the school, and they went to the head of the English department, who was a Jewish woman and a great teacher. Steve remembers the event in these words:

> She (the head of the English department) looked up and saw me standing there by my daughter and could tell that Robin was about to cry. There were some students standing around and, because the teacher didn't want Robin to be embarrassed, she dismissed the students saying, "I want to talk to these people alone." As soon as the students left and the door was closed, Robin began to cry. I said, "I'm here to get my daughter out of that English class. It's too difficult for her. The problem with my daughter is that she's too conscientious. So, can you put her into a regular English class?" The teacher said, "Mr. Brown, I understand." Then she looked at Robin and said, "Can I talk to Robin for a minute?" I said, "Sure." She said, "Robin, I know how you feel. What if I promised you an A no matter what you did in the class? If I gave you an A before you even started, would you be willing to take the class?" My daughter is not dumb! She started sniffling and said, "Well, I think I could do that." The teacher said, "I'm going to give you an A in the class. You already have an A, so you can go to class.

Later the teacher explained to Steve what she had done. She explained how she took away the threat of a bad grade so that Robin could learn English literature. Robin ended up making straight A's on her own in that class.[2]

That's how God deals with us. Because of Christ's finished work, Christians already have an A. The threat of failure, judgment, and condemnation has been removed. We're in—forever! Nothing we do will make our grade better, and nothing we do will make our grade worse. In his life, by his death, and with his resurrection, Christ our substitute secured for us the *everything*, the A, that we come into this world longing for and yet are incapable of securing for ourselves. All the pardon, the approval, the purpose, the freedom, the rescue, the meaning, the righteousness, the cleansing, the significance, the worth, and the affection we crave and need are already ours in Christ. We don't need to add anything to it. The operative power that makes you a Christian is the same operative power that keeps you a Christian: the unconditional, unqualified, undeserved, unrestrained grace of God in the completed work of Christ.

As I said, the banner under which Christians live reads, "It is finished." So relax, and rejoice. Jesus plus nothing equals everything; everything minus Jesus equals nothing.

You're free!

TWENTY-SIX BOOKS
ON THE GOSPEL

As I've said before, I once assumed (along with the vast majority of professing Christians) that the gospel was simply what non-Christians must believe in order to be saved, while afterward we advance to deeper theological waters. But I've come to realize that once God rescues sinners, his plan isn't to steer them beyond the gospel but to move them more deeply into it. The gospel, in other words, isn't just the power of God to save you; it's the power of God to grow you once you're saved.

This idea that the gospel is just as much for Christians as it is for non-Christians may seem like a new idea to many but, in fact, it is really a very old idea.

There have been many books (beneath the Bible, of course) that have helped me as I've wrestled with how God intends the reality of the gospel to shape and liberate us at every point and in every way. The following list of books is not exhaustive, but if you read them, you will be moving in the right direction toward a better, more biblical understanding of the gospel and how to preach it to yourself every day.

No one will agree with all of the content in these books. In fact, some of these books represent different perspectives on the finer points of gospel-based sanctification. Some of these authors disagree with one another on some things. But reading them all and wrestling with them all will make you wise.

I also urge you to be a diligent and intentional reader. Highlight and underline key phrases and sentences and make notes in the margins. As C. S. Lewis said, "The best way to read is with book in lap, pen in hand, and pipe in teeth." So enjoy these books—but easy on the tobacco.

My prayer for you (and for the whole church) is that as you come to a better understanding of the length and breadth of the gospel you will be recaptured everyday by the "God of great expenditure" who gave everything that we might possess all.

Alexander, Donald, ed. *Christian Spirituality: Five Views of Sanctification.* Downers Grove, IL: InterVarsity, 1988.

Bridges, Jerry. *The Discipline of Grace: God's Role and Our Role in the Pursuit of Holiness.* Colorado Springs, CO: NavPress, 1994.

_____. *Transforming Grace: Living Confidently in God's Unfailing Love.* Colorado Springs, CO: NavPress, 2008.

Brown, Steve. *A Scandalous Freedom: The Radical Nature of the Gospel.* New York: Howard, 2004.

Chapell, Bryan. *Holiness by Grace: Delighting in the Joy That Is Our Strength.* Wheaton, IL: Crossway, 2003.

Clark, R. Scott, ed. *Covenant, Justification, and Pastoral Ministry: Essays by the Faculty of Westminster Seminary.* Phillipsburg, NJ: P&R, 2007.

Dawson, Gerrit Scott. *Called by a New Name: Becoming What God Has Promised.* Nashville: Upper Room, 2008.

Ferguson, Sinclair. *In Christ Alone: Living the Gospel Centered Life.* Lake Mary, FL: Reformation Trust, 2007.

Fitzpatrick, Elyse. *Because He Loves Me: How Christ Transforms Our Daily Life.* Wheaton, IL: Crossway, 2008.

Fitzpatrick, Elyse, and Dennis Johnson. *Counsel From the Cross: Connecting Broken People to the Love of Christ.* Wheaton, IL: Crossway, 2008.

Forde, Gerhard O. *Justification by Faith: A Matter of Death and Life.* Mifflintown, PA: Sigler, 1991.

_____. *On Being a Theologian of the Cross: Reflections on Luther's Heidelberg Disputation, 1518.* Grand Rapids, MI: Eerdmans, 1997.

Hedges, Brian. *Christ Formed in You: The Power of the Gospel for Personal Change*. Wapwallopen, PA: Shepherd, 2010.

Horton, Michael. *Christless Christianity: The Alternative Gospel of the American Church*. Grand Rapids, MI: Baker, 2008.

_____. *The Gospel-Driven Life: Being Good News People in a Bad News World*. Grand Rapids, MI: Baker, 2009.

Keller, Tim. *Counterfeit Gods: The Empty Promises of Money, Sex, and Power, and the Only Hope That Matters*. New York: Dutton, 2009.

_____. *The Prodigal God: Recovering the Heart of the Christian Faith*. New York: Dutton, 2008.

Marshall, Walter. *The Gospel Mystery of Sanctification*. Mulberry, IN: Sovereign Grace, 2001.

Miller, Rose Marie. *From Fear to Freedom: Living as Sons and Daughters of God*. Colorado Springs, CO: Shaw, 1994.

Senkbeil, Harold L. *Dying to Live: The Power of Forgiveness*. St. Louis, MO: Concordia, 1994.

Smith, Scotty. *Everyday Prayers: 365 Days to a Gospel-Centered Faith*. Grand Rapids, MI: Baker, 2011.

_____. *The Reign of Grace: The Delights and Demands of God's Love*. West Monroe, LA: Howard, 2003.

Tripp, Paul. *Broken Down House: Living Productively in a World Gone Bad*. Wapwallopen, PA: Shepherd, 2009.

Walther, C. F. W. *God's No and God's Yes: The Proper Distinction between Law and Gospel*. St. Louis, MO: Concordia, 1973.

Zahl, Paul. *Grace in Practice: A Theology of Everyday Life*. Grand Rapids, MI: Eerdmans, 2007.

_____. *Who Will Deliver Us: The Present Power of the Death of Christ*. Eugene, OR: Wipf & Stock, 2008.

NOTES

CHAPTER 2: WANTING IT ALL

1. Pascal's *Pensées*, trans. W. F. Trotter (Chicago: University of Chicago Press, 1990), no. 425.

2. Paul Tripp, *A Shelter in the Time of Storm: Meditations on God in Trouble* (Wheaton, IL: Crossway, 2009), 33–34.

3. C. S. Lewis, *Mere Christianity* (New York: Macmillan, 1952), 120.

CHAPTER 3: STILL SEARCHING

1. C. S. Lewis, *The Screwtape Letters* (New York: MacMillan, 1945), 126.

2. Michael Horton, *Christless Christianity: The Alternative Gospel of the American Church* (Grand Rapids, MI: Baker, 2008).

3. http://www.desiringgod.org/blog/posts/the-gracious-rescue-of-surprise.

CHAPTER 4: BLACK HOLES

1. A. W. Pink, *Studies in the Scriptures,* vol. 8 (Mulberry, IN: Sovereign Grace, 2001), 376.

2. Gerhard Forde, *A More Radical Gospel* (Grand Rapids, MI: Eerdmans, 2004), 142.

3. From Mark Driscoll's sermon "Jesus the Sabbath Lord," March 28, 2010, at Mars Hill Church, Seattle; the list is summarized at http://theresurgence.com/2010/04/06/how-to-become-a-legalist.

4. Leo Tolstoy, *A Confession and Other Religious Writings* (Digireads.com, 2010), 15.

CHAPTER 5: JESUS, ALL AND MORE

1. John Piper, *Desiring God: Meditations of a Christian Hedonist*, rev. ed. (Colorado Springs, CO: Multnomah, 2011), 13.

2. Matthew Henry, *Commentary on the Whole Bible,* vol. 2 (1708; repr. Old Tappan, NJ: Revell), commenting on Nehemiah 8:10–11; p. 1096.

3. Curtis Vaughan, *Colossians*, vol. 11, Expositors Bible Commentary, ed. Frank E. Gabelein (Grand Rapids, MI: Zondervan, 1978), 184.

4. Ibid., 185.

5. John Calvin, *Commentaries on the Epistles of Paul the Apostle to the Philippians, Colossians, and Thessalonians,* Calvin's Commentaries, trans. John Pringle (Grand Rapids, MI: Eerdmans, 1948), at Col. 1:14.

6. Ibid., at Col. 1:15.

7. Vaughan, *Colossians*, 181.

8. C. S. Lewis, "The Weight of Glory," in *The Weight of Glory and Other Addresses*, ed. W. Hooper (New York: Simon & Schuster, 1996), 25–26.

CHAPTER 6: NEWS—THE BIGGEST AND BEST

1. Paul F. M. Zahl, *Who Will Deliver Us: The Present Power of the Death of Christ* (Eugene, OR: Wipf & Stock, 1983), 76

CHAPTER 7: FULLY EXPOSED

1. Timothy Keller, *Counterfeit Gods: The Empty Promises of Money, Sex, and Power, and the Only Hope That Matters* (New York: Dutton, 2009), xvii–xix.

2. Ibid., 3.

3. Michael Horton, *Christless Christianity: The Alternative Gospel of the American Church* (Grand Rapids, MI: Baker, 2008), 17–18.

4. Michael Horton, *The Gospel-Driven Life: Being Good News People in a Bad News Life* (Grand Rapids, MI: Baker, 2009), 150, 152.

5. Jerry Bridges, *The Gospel in Real Life: Turn to the Liberating Power of the Cross . . . Every Day* (Colorado Springs, CO: NavPress, 2002), 11.

6. Elyse Fitzpatrick, *Because He Loves Me: How Christ Transforms Our Daily Life* (Wheaton, IL: Crossway, 2008), 44; emphasis original.

7. Horton, *Christless Christianity*, 243.

8. Ibid., 61.

9. Ibid.

10. Ibid., 240.

11. Horton, *The Gospel-Driven Life*, 149–50.

12. Ibid., 145.

CHAPTER 8: OUT OF THE SHADOWS

1. C. S. Lewis, *God in the Dock: Essays on Theology and Ethics* (Grand Rapids, MI: Eerdmans, 1994), 180.

2. Harold Senkbeil, *Dying to Live: The Power of Forgiveness* (St. Louis, MO: Concordia, 1994), 13.

3. Harold Senkbeil, in *Justified: Modern Reformation Essays on the Doctrine of Justification*, vol. 1, ed. Ryan Glomsrud and Michael Horton (CreateSpace, 2010), n. p.

4. Timothy Keller, *Counterfeit Gods: The Empty Promises of Money, Sex, and Power, and the Only Hope That Matters* (New York: Dutton, 2009), 172.

5. Paul F. M. Zahl, *Who Will Deliver Us: The Present Power of the Death of Christ* (Eugene, OR: Wipf & Stock, 2008), 10.

6. Elyse Fitzpatrick, *Because He Loves Me: How Christ Transforms Our Daily Life* (Wheaton, IL: Crossway, 2008), 193.

7. See Gerhard Forde, *A More Radical Gospel: Essays on Eschatology, Authority, Atonement, and Ecumenism* (Grand Rapids, MI: Eerdmans, 2004), 140.

CHAPTER 9: EVERYTHING NOW, AND MORE COMING

1. Michael Horton, *The Gospel-Driven Life: Being Good News People in a Bad News World* (Grand Rapids, MI: Baker, 2009), 133, 144.

2. Paul F. M. Zahl, *Who Will Deliver Us: The Present Power of the Death of Christ* (Eugene, OR: Wipf & Stock, 2008), 11.

3. Jerry Bridges and Bob Bevington, *The Bookends of the Christian Life* (Wheaton, IL: Crossway, 2009), 24–26.

4. John Murray, *Redemption Accomplished and Applied* (Grand Rapids, MI: Eerdmans, 1955), 21–22.

5. Michael Horton, "Obedience Is Better Than Sacrifice," in *The Law Is Not of Faith: Essays on Works and Grace in the Mosaic Covenant* (Phillipsburg, NJ: P&R, 2009), 320.

6. "O the Deep, Deep Love of Jesus," words by Samuel Trevor Francis, ca. 1890.

CHAPTER 10: OUR FULL RESPONSE

1. *ESV Study Bible* (Wheaton, IL: Crossway, 2008), at Col. 1:23.

2. John Calvin, *Commentaries on the Epistles of Paul the Apostle to the Philippians, Colossians, and Thessalonians,* Calvin's Commentaries, trans. John Pringle (Grand Rapids, MI: Eerdmans, 1948), at Col. 2:6.

3. Ibid., at Col. 2:7.

4. As included in John Piper's sermon "Called to Suffer and Rejoice: To Finish the Aim of Christ's Afflictions," August 30, 1992; http://www.desiringgod. org/resource-library/sermons/called-to-suffer-and-rejoice-to-finish-the-aim-of-christs-afflictions. Piper credits the story as follows: Michael Card, "Wounded in the House of Friends," *Virtue,* March/April 1991, pp. 28–29, 69. The story is also included in Michael Card's *Immanuel: Reflections on the Life of Christ* (Nashville: Nelson, 1990), 172–74.

CHAPTER 11: IN THE NOW

1. Gerhard Forde, *Justification by Faith* (Mifflintown, PA: Sigler, 1991), 51.

2. Quoted in Dane Ortlund, "The Radical Gospel, Defiant and Free," as featured at the Gospel Coalition website, http://thegospelcoalition.org/blogs/tgc/2011/01/27/the-radical-gospel-defiant-and-free/.

3. Donald Alexander, ed., *Christian Spirituality: Five Views on Sanctification* (Downers Grove, IL: IVP Academic, 1988), 32.

4. Sinclair Ferguson, in words featured on the Monergism website, http://www.monergism.com/monthly_focus/gospel_centered_life.php.

5. Sinclair Ferguson, in an interview with C. J. Mahaney (http://sovereign graceministries.org/blogs/cj-mahaney/category/Introspection.aspx). Ferguson cites these words as coming from "a course on the doctrine of the church and the sacraments."

6. Michael Horton, "Does Justification Still Matter?" *Modern Reformation,* vol. 16 (Sept./Oct. 2007), 11.

7. Michael Horton, *The Gospel-Driven Life: Being Good News People in a Bad News World* (Grand Rapids, MI: Baker, 2009), 150.

8. Elyse Fitzpatrick, *Because He Loves Me: How Christ Transforms Our Daily Life* (Wheaton, IL: Crossway, 2008), 110.

9. Dane Ortlund, "The Radical Gospel, Defiant and Free," as featured at the Gospel Coalition website, http://thegospelcoalition.org/blogs/tgc/2011/01/27/the-radical-gospel-defiant-and-free/.

10. Charles H. Spurgeon, in his sermon "Repentance after Conversion," June 12, 1887; sermon #2419 in the *Metropolitan Tabernacle Pulpit;* Spurgeon Gems website, http://www.spurgeongems.org/vols40-42/chs2419.pdf.

CHAPTER 12: ALL GLORIOUS

1. As retold by Ray Ortlund, http://thegospelcoalition.org/blogs/rayortlund/?s=Chrysostom; with details from R. Kent Hughes in *Romans: Righteousness from Heaven,* Preaching the Word (Wheaton, IL: Crossway, 1991), 171; further clarified in Ortlund's personal conversation with Tom Nettles, church historian at The Southern Baptist Theological Seminary, Louisville, KY.

2. Steve Brown, *Born Free: How to Find Radical Freedom and Infectious Joy in an Authentic Faith* (Maitland, FL: Key Life Network, 1993), 108.

GENERAL INDEX

SCRIPTURE INDEX

ADDITIONAL RESOURCES

TWITTER
twitter.com/pastortullian

SERMONS
Pastor Tullian Tchividjian's sermons may be downloaded for free on the church's website (www.crpc.org) or from iTunes. They are also available on CD through the resource ministry LIBERATE. To request a sermon on CD, please e-mail LIBERATE@crpc.org.

Steps to Peace With God

1. God's Purpose: Peace and Life

God loves you and wants you to experience peace and life—abundant and eternal.

The Bible Says ...

"We have peace with God through our Lord Jesus Christ." *Romans 5:1, NKJV*

"For God so loved the world that He gave His only begotten Son, that whoever believes in Him should not perish but have everlasting life." *John 3:16, NKJV*

"I have come that they may have life, and that they may have it more abundantly." *John 10:10, NKJV*

Since God planned for us to have peace and the abundant life right now, why are most people not having this experience?

2. Our Problem: Separation From God

God created us in His own image to have an abundant life. He did not make us as robots to automatically love and obey Him, but gave us a will and a freedom of choice.

We chose to disobey God and go our own willful way. We still make this choice today. This results in separation from God.

The Bible Says ...

"For all have sinned and fall short of the glory of God." *Romans 3:23, NKJV*

"For the wages of sin is death, but the gift of God is eternal life in Christ Jesus our Lord." *Romans 6:23, NKJV*

Our choice results in separation from God.

People (Sinful)   God (Holy)

Our Attempts

Through the ages, individuals have tried in many ways to bridge this gap ... without success ...

The Bible says ...

"There is a way that seems right to a man, but its end is the way of death."
Proverbs 14:12, NKJV

"But your iniquities have separated you from your God; and your sins have hidden His face from you, so that He will not hear."
Isaiah 59:2, NKJV

There is only one remedy for this problem of separation.

3. God's Remedy: The Cross

Jesus Christ is the only answer to this problem. He died on the cross and rose from the grave, paying the penalty for our sin and bridging the gap between God and people.

The Bible says ...

"For there is one God and one Mediator between God and men, the Man Christ Jesus."
1 Timothy 2:5, NKJV

"For Christ also suffered once for sins, the just for the unjust, that He might bring us to God."
1 Peter 3:18, NKJV

"But God demonstrates His own love toward us, in that while we were still sinners, Christ died for us." *Romans 5:8, NKJV*

God has provided the only way ... we must make the choice ...

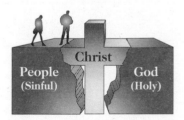

4. Our Response: Receive Christ

We must trust Jesus Christ and receive Him by personal invitation.

The Bible Says ...

"Behold, I stand at the door and knock. If anyone hears My voice and opens the door, I will come in to him and dine with him, and he with Me." *Revelation 3:20, NKJV*

"But as many as received Him, to them He gave the right to become children of God, to those who believe in His name." *John 1:12, NKJV*

"If you confess with your mouth the Lord Jesus and believe in your heart that God has raised Him from the dead, you will be saved." *Romans 10:9, NKJV*

Are you here ... or here?

Is there any good reason why you cannot receive Jesus Christ right now?

How to Receive Christ:

1. Admit your need (say, "I am a sinner").
2. Be willing to turn from your sins (repent) and ask for God's forgiveness.
3. Believe that Jesus Christ died for you on the cross and rose from the grave.
4. Through prayer, invite Jesus Christ to come in and control your life through the Holy Spirit (receive Jesus as Lord and Savior).

What to Pray:

Dear Lord Jesus,
  I know that I am a sinner, and I ask for Your forgiveness. I believe You died for my sins and rose from the dead. I turn from my sins and invite You to come into my heart and life. I want to trust and follow You as my Lord and Savior.

In Your Name, amen.

_____   _____
Date   Signature

GOD'S ASSURANCE: HIS WORD

IF YOU PRAYED THIS PRAYER,

THE BIBLE SAYS ...

"For 'whoever calls on the name of the Lord shall be saved.'"
Romans 10:13, NKJV

Did you sincerely ask Jesus Christ to come into your life?
Where is He right now? What has He given you?

"For by grace you have been saved through faith, and that not of
yourselves; it is the gift of God, not of works, lest anyone should boast."
Ephesians 2:8–9, NKJV

THE BIBLE SAYS ...

"He who has the Son has life; he who does not have the Son of God does
not have life. These things I have written to you who believe in the name of
the Son of God, that you may know that you have eternal life, and that you
may continue to believe in the name of the Son of God."
1 John 5:12–13, NKJV

Receiving Christ, we are born into God's family through the
supernatural work of the Holy Spirit who indwells every believer.
This is called regeneration or the "new birth."

This is just the beginning of a wonderful new life in Christ. To deepen
this relationship you should:

1. Read your Bible every day to know Christ better.
2. Talk to God in prayer every day.
3. Tell others about Christ.
4. Worship, fellowship, and serve with other Christians in a church where Christ
   is preached.
5. As Christ's representative in a needy world, demonstrate your new life by
   your love and concern for others.

God bless you as you do.

Billy Graham

If you want further help in the decision you have made, write to:
Billy Graham Evangelistic Association
1 Billy Graham Parkway, Charlotte, NC 28201-0001

1-877-2GRAHAM (1-877-247-2426)
BillyGraham.org/commitment

COME AWAY ...

Everyone enters at the foot of the cross.

Throughout their tour, they encounter the Gospel at every turn. Every aspect of the Billy Graham Library in Charlotte, N.C., is designed to proclaim God's love and forgiveness. Come experience this journey of faith for yourself.

The
BILLY
GRAHAM
Library